FEASTS

SABRINA GHAYOUR
FEASTS

MIDDLE EASTERN FOOD TO SAVOR & SHARE

weldon**owen**

weldon**owen**

Published in North America by Weldon Owen
1045 Sansome Street, San Francisco, CA 94111
www.weldonowen.com
Weldon Owen is a division of Bonnier Publishing USA

First published in Great Britain in 2017 by
Mitchell Beazley, a division of
Octopus Publishing Group Ltd

Text copyright © Sabrina Ghayour 2017
Photography copyright © Kris Kirkham 2017
Design and layout copyright © Octopus Publishing Group 2017

ISBN 978-1-68188-374-8

Library of Congress Cataloging-in-Publication data is available

Printed and bound in China

This edition printed in 2017

10 9 8 7 6 5 4 3 2 1

"Life is a feast, and all who eat and drink with me,
and savor food as they savor life,
are those who matter most."

CONTENTS

INTRODUCTION

As a child, growing up in a Persian household means endless parties, which we call *mehmooni*. My family regularly played host, and we would frequently attend big family gatherings, both indoors and outdoors. Those parties, and the feasts we shared at them, became a huge and influential part of my childhood. The overwhelming noise of people animatedly greeting one another as they embraced, and the loud infectious laughter and warmth that were shared, are things I will never forget. I am so grateful to have been part of something that I now treasure as a golden era in my life.

I remember arriving at parties and being immediately seduced by the exotic smells that filled the house. I would watch platter after platter of elaborately presented dishes emerge from the kitchen, being carried carefully to the table. Once laid out, they would form part of an enormous, colorful spread that would soon be descended upon by dozens of people at once, yet seemed never-ending in supply. When you are a kid at only about table height, you have a major advantage over everyone else—sneaking away little bites before the grown-ups were ready to eat was not terribly uncommon in my case.

Feasting plays an important role not only in Persian culture but also in that of the entire Middle East. In ancient terms, what was served and how many exotic dishes and ingredients were offered might have sealed the fate of an entire empire! Feasts have always played an important role in the history of empires across the globe, and the breaking of bread and sharing of meals have long played a part in uniting cultures, communities, and families by bringing people together in a convivial and uninhibited way, where all differences can be left aside at the table. Today, time plays a key factor in whether or not we entertain and we don't seem to entertain as often as we used to— life seems to get in the way.

I thought carefully about the types of recipes I wanted to share with you in this book, and the chapters are dedicated to creating meals that are conducive to the way we live our lives today. I've suggested a menu within each chapter, but as the biggest rule breaker of them all, I am the kind of person who will choose a recipe from every chapter and throw them all together for a feast, so I would encourage you to make your own choices and do the same.

As is the case in my previous books, the recipes I offer are straightforward and, for the most part, not too labor-intensive (and, in some cases, really quite easy to make) but deliver big in the flavor sweepstakes, even if they contain only a handful of ingredients. It seems the older I get, the more I crave simplicity over refinement and fuss.

Many of you are now very familiar with the Middle East and its abundance of flavor, color, and ingredients. While my recipes are very much my own creations and the kind of food I like to eat at home, they remain heavily inspired by my travels and the wonderful produce and ingredients from around the world. There will always be plenty of Persian flavor inspiration to help you create a feast that is perfect for your table, no matter what the occasion may be.

The recipes in this book may be new, but my ethos remains the same—no ingredient is truly ever essential (unless you are baking, when sometimes science takes precedence over creativity), and there is always room to chop and change ingredients and use what you have or what you can get a hold of. In most cases, omitting an ingredient won't affect the flavor or nature of a dish, so don't be afraid to skip or substitute an ingredient here or there. I realize how many people are afraid to deviate from a recipe for fear of failure, but I can assure you that I myself am not the type of cook who sticks to a recipe 100 percent of the time, and generally it works, so don't be afraid to experiment.

Whether you follow my chapter and menu suggestions or if, like me, you prefer to pick and choose recipes from across the board to create your own special feast, may your feasts always be plentiful—I hope this book provides you with easy inspiration to make cooking less of a chore and more of a joy.

BREAKFAST
&
BRUNCH

It has long been said that breakfast is the most important meal of the day. Even the word itself, when broken down into "break" and "fast," reminds us of its actual purpose. Most of us have our own preferences and rituals when we have a little more time on our hands rather than just enough time to smear a thin layer of jam across a piece of toast and fly out the door with it dangling from our mouths.

I will let you in on a secret… I am a strange one when it comes to leisurely breakfast feasting, in that I need to start the day with a ritual of two cups of coffee, then some toast. Within a couple of hours, I am then ready for a heartier breakfast or brunch. So, basically, I am a two-breakfast kind of gal. Also, what I eat for breakfast is very much mood-driven. Consistency and necessity never play a role in my selections. I can hop erratically and wildly around the food groups and eat everything from leftover curry and roasted potatoes to cold clams with chile and garlic or just a piece of ham. I am aware this is not something most people do, but it does say something about my tastes—that I veer mostly toward savory dishes for brunch.

When you have a family or group to feed for breakfast or brunch, you really want to put your energy and effort into making dishes that have interesting but not too many overpowering flavors, as subtlety goes a long way at this time of the day. Subtlety has many guises and need never be boring, familiar, or predictable—I like to serve the kind of dishes that provide a wake-up call, flavor-wise, to those who need it, and that set you up for the day, not just the morning, with flavors that are often bold but always balanced.

Choose one recipe or choose them all—there is something for everyone in this chapter, and you can throw in a few of your own favorite breakfast essentials. The point here is to take what you like and combine it with what you have and what your favorite staples are… that is always the winning formula for any great meal, no matter what time of day.

BREAKFAST & BRUNCH

MENU

Cheddar & feta frittata with peppers, herbs & pul biber (page 18)

Sausage, potato, pepper & onion bake with yogurt & chile sauce (page 22)

Whipped ricotta & fig toasts with candied chile bacon (page 30)

Caramelized banana crêpes with pistachios & honey (page 33)

Accompaniments:
Tea, coffee & fruit juice

GOAT CHEESE & FILO PIES

with orange, pistachio & oregano

MAKES 8

¾ cup pistachio nuts, finely chopped

14 oz soft goat cheese

finely grated zest of 2 large unwaxed
    oranges

2 heaping teaspoons dried oregano

freshly ground black pepper

3 sheets of filo pastry

4 tablespoons unsalted butter, melted, plus
    more for greasing

1 tablespoon nigella seeds

honey, for drizzling (optional)

Preheat the oven to 425°F. Grease an 8-cup muffin pan with melted butter.

Put the pistachios and goat cheese in a large bowl. Add the orange zest, oregano, and a generous amount of black pepper and mash together using a fork until the mixture is evenly combined. Divide the mixture equally into 8 portions.

Cut each filo pastry sheet roughly into 8 squares, each about 5 inches square. Overlap 1 pastry square with another to make an 8-pointed star. Repeat to make 8 stars. Push the stars into the muffin-pan cups and brush with melted butter. Spoon 1 portion of the filling into each filo star and press gently on the filling.

Take 1 of the remaining pastry squares and crinkle it up in your hand. Place it on top of one of the pie fillings, brush with butter, then fold over the pastry edges to seal the pie. Brush the edges with more butter and sprinkle over a few nigella seeds. Repeat until all the pies are topped and sealed.

Bake until deeply golden brown, about 25 minutes. Drizzle each pie with a little honey if desired, then serve.

CHEDDAR & FETA FRITTATA

with peppers, herbs & pul biber

SERVES 4–6

vegetable oil

½ red pepper, cut into ½-inch strips, then diced into ½-inch pieces

½ green pepper, cut into ½-inch strips, then diced into ½-inch pieces

4 spring onions, thinly sliced from root to tip

8 oz feta cheese, broken into ½-inch chunks

4 oz mature Cheddar cheese, grated

1 tablespoon pul biber chile flakes

½ small bunch (about ½ oz) dill, finely chopped

½ small bunch (about ½ oz) fresh cilantro, finely chopped

8 large eggs, beaten

Maldon sea salt flakes and freshly ground black pepper

Preheat the oven to 425°F.

Drizzle a little oil into a large, ovenproof frying pan and set it over medium-high heat. When the oil is hot, add the peppers and fry for 1 minute, stirring to prevent them from taking on color or burning. Mix in the spring onions, feta, Cheddar, pul biber, dill, and cilantro.

Season the beaten eggs well with salt and pepper and pour them over the ingredients in the pan, then shake the pan to ensure the egg spreads evenly around the pan and coats all the contents. Cook until you see the edges of the frittata begin to solidify, about 2 minutes, then transfer the pan to the oven and bake until the frittata is cooked, 10–12 minutes; insert a knife into the center to ensure the egg is cooked through. Either slide or flip the frittata onto a plate and serve, or serve straight from the pan. The leftovers are delicious served at room temperature.

SPICY TAMARIND BEANS

SERVES 6–8

1 lb dried navy beans

2–3 tablespoons vegetable oil

2 large onions, finely chopped or minced
in a food processor

2 fat garlic cloves, crushed

1 tablespoon cocoa powder

2 teaspoons ground cinnamon

2 teaspoons ground cumin

1 teaspoon cayenne pepper

1 can (14½ oz) chopped tomatoes

½ cup tamarind paste (the paste should
be the consistency of a ketchup)

4 tablespoons brown sugar

4 tablespoons red wine vinegar

Maldon sea salt flakes and freshly ground
black pepper

2 cups boiling water

toasted bread, to serve

Soak the beans overnight, then drain and rinse well. Transfer the beans to a large saucepan, cover with cold water, and boil over medium-high heat until just tender, about 45 minutes. Drain and rinse well to remove excess starch.

Heat the oil in a large saucepan over medium-high heat. Add the onions and fry until translucent and the edges start to brown, 6–8 minutes. Add the beans, garlic, cocoa powder, cinnamon, cumin, and cayenne pepper and stir to coat the beans well. Next, add the tomatoes, tamarind paste, sugar, and red wine vinegar and season generously with salt and black pepper. Pour in the 2 cups of boiling water, reduce the heat to low, and simmer until the beans are soft (taste a bean to check), 1–1½ hours. Check the seasoning and adjust to your taste.

Serve with toasted bread. This dish is great served with bacon or sausages.

TIP

Tamarind paste comes in different consistencies and concentrates. This recipe is best made with a paste the consistency of thick ketchup—it should not be dense or sticky. If your paste is the thicker, more concentrated variety, simply add less of it and add more sweetness to balance the flavors and to suit your preference.

SAUSAGE, POTATO, PEPPER & ONION BAKE

with yogurt & chile sauce

SERVES 4–6

2 teaspoons cumin seeds

2 teaspoons coriander seeds

1 tablespoon sweet paprika

2 tablespoons pul biber chile flakes

1 lb sausages (preferably with a high meat content)

3 tablespoons garlic oil

Maldon sea salt flakes and freshly ground black pepper

2 large potatoes, parboiled with skin on and cut into ½-inch-thick slices

½ lb small peppers or 1 large red and 1 large green pepper, cored, deseeded and cut lengthwise into 1-inch-thick strips

2 large red onions, quartered and each quarter halved

TO SERVE
¾ cup thick Greek yogurt
Sriracha

Heat a large frying pan over medium-high heat, add the cumin and coriander seeds, and toast, shaking the pan until they release their aroma and begin to brown a little, taking care not to let them burn, about 1 minute. Transfer the seeds to a mortar and pestle and crush them very roughly, just to break them. Transfer to a bowl and combine with the paprika and pul biber.

Using the same frying pan you used to toast the seeds, fry the sausages over high heat until they start to brown on all sides, 6–8 minutes; you don't need to fully cook them in the pan as they will finish cooking in the oven later. Remove from the heat, cut each sausage into 3 slices diagonally, and set aside.

Preheat the oven to its highest temperature. Line a baking sheet with parchment paper.

Brush the paper with 1 tablespoon of the garlic oil and season the base with salt and pepper. Lay the potato slices on the parchment paper and season again with salt and pepper and one-third of the spice mixture. Evenly distribute the sausages, peppers, and onions among the potato slices. Reserve a little of the spice mix for sprinkling, then drizzle over the remaining garlic oil and spice mix and season generously with salt and pepper.

Bake until the peppers are nicely browned and the sausages are cooked through, 16–18 minutes.

Serve with dollops of thick Greek yogurt, a good drizzle of Sriracha (or other chile sauce), and a sprinkling of the reserved spice mix. This dish goes well with simple fried or scrambled eggs.

GREEN GINGER LEMONADE

SERVES 4

ice cubes

1 small bunch (about 1 oz) mint,
    stalks removed

½ small bunch (about ½ oz) dill,
    roughly chopped

2-inch piece fresh ginger,
    peeled and very finely chopped

6 tablespoons superfine sugar,
    plus more to taste

finely grated zest and juice of 3 lemons

4 cups tepid water

Fill a blender half full with ice cubes and add the mint leaves, dill, ginger, sugar, lemon zest, and juice along with 2 cups of the tepid water. Blitz until the mixture is well blended.

Transfer the liquid to a large pitcher, add the remaining 2 cups water, and stir. Check the sweetness and adjust to taste.

Put some ice cubes into 4 highball glasses, top up with the green lemonade, and serve.

ZA'ATAR-CRUMBED
HALLOUMI

SERVES 4–5

vegetable oil

2 x 8-oz blocks of halloumi cheese

1 large egg, beaten

6 tablespoons fine bread crumbs

4 tablespoons za'atar

Pour enough oil into a large, deep-sided frying pan to fill it to a depth of about 1 inch. Heat the oil over high heat. Line a plate with a double layer of paper towels.

Slice each block of halloumi into 5 even slices, each about ½ inch thick. Put the beaten egg into a shallow bowl. In a separate bowl, mix the bread crumbs and za'atar together. Dip each slice of halloumi into the egg to give it a generous coating, then roll it in the spiced bread crumbs. When fully coated on all sides, fry the halloumi in the hot oil until the crumbs turn golden brown, about 1 minute. Transfer to the paper towel–lined plate to drain the excess oil, then serve immediately.

PEA PASTIZZI

MAKES 10

olive oil

1 large onion, very finely chopped

2 fat garlic cloves, crushed

2 cups frozen peas, thawed

1 tablespoon medium-spiced curry powder

½ teaspoon freshly ground black pepper

Maldon sea salt flakes

1½ tablespoons unsalted butter

1 sheet of frozen all-butter puff pastry, thawed

1 large egg, beaten

Drizzle a little olive oil into a frying pan set over medium-high heat. When the oil is hot, add the onion and cook for a few minutes until softened and starting to color around the edges. Add the garlic and cook until the onion and garlic begin to color and are cooked through, about 1 minute. Stir in the peas, curry powder, pepper, butter, and a generous amount of salt (as peas are very sweet and need to be seasoned well). Cook for about 5 minutes, mashing the peas roughly as you stir, until they are cooked through. Remove the pan from the heat and leave to cool.

Preheat the oven to 400°F. Line a baking sheet with parchment paper.

Place the sheet of puff pastry on a clean work surface with its paper lining underneath it. Using a sharp knife, slice the sheet into 10 equal rectangles. Using your fingers, form the cooled pea mixture into 10 sausage-shaped portions. Press 1 portion onto each rectangle of pastry. Gather the 2 ends of the pastry rectangle and fold them over the ends of the sausage, then roll up the filling in the pastry and pinch the pastry to seal in the filling. Seal any gaps in the pastry by carefully pinching them shut. Place the roll on the prepared baking sheet with the sealed side facing down. Repeat with the remaining pastry rectangles and portions of filling. Brush the rolls with the beaten egg and bake until crisp and golden, about 25 minutes. Serve immediately. These rolls are also great served at room temperature.

APPLE, CINNAMON & GOLDEN RAISIN LOAF

with nigella honey butter

MAKES 1 LARGE LOAF

¼ oz package of instant yeast

⅓ cup lukewarm water

½ cup milk, at room temperature

1 egg

⅓ cup superfine sugar

2¾ oz golden raisins

1 heaping tablespoon ground cinnamon

4 tablespoons unsalted butter, melted, plus more for greasing

1 Braeburn apple, coarsely grated

pinch of Maldon sea salt flakes

4 cups bread flour, plus more as required

FOR THE NIGELLA HONEY BUTTER

2 tablespoons nigella seeds

6 tablespoons unsalted butter

3 tablespoons honey

Dissolve the yeast in the lukewarm water and leave for 10 minutes to activate.

Put the milk, egg, sugar, raisins, cinnamon, 3 tablespoons of the melted butter, the grated apple, and salt into a large mixing bowl and mix well. Stir in the activated yeast liquid, then add the flour. Blend until a slightly sticky dough is formed. Use a little more flour to help you bring the dough together, then knead it for a couple of minutes. Put the dough into a bowl, cover it with a clean kitchen towel, and leave it somewhere warm to rest for 1½ hours.

To make the nigella honey butter, blitz the nigella seeds using a spice grinder or food processor until fine, or grind them using a mortar and pestle. Put the butter in a bowl, add the nigella seed powder and honey, and work them into the butter until evenly combined. Refrigerate until 15 minutes before needed.

When the resting time has elapsed, lightly grease a 5 x 9 x 3–inch loaf pan. Carefully remove the dough (using a little flour to extract it from the bowl, if needed) and shape it into a long loaf. Tuck the 2 long edges underneath so the top forms a smooth dome. Gently push the dough into the prepared pan and leave to proof (uncovered) in a warm place for 20 minutes.

Preheat the oven to 400°F.

When the dough has risen in the pan, brush it with the remaining 1 tablespoon melted butter. Bake until the top is deeply golden brown and the loaf sounds hollow when tapped, 45–50 minutes. Remove from the pan and allow to cool completely, then serve the loaf with the nigella honey butter.

WHIPPED RICOTTA
& FIG TOASTS

with candied chile bacon

MAKES 4

½ lb thick-cut unsmoked bacon
(approximately 14 slices)
1 tablespoon pul biber chile flakes,
plus more to serve
4 tablespoons honey
8 oz ricotta cheese
1 heaping teaspoon dried thyme,
plus more to serve
zest of 1 unwaxed orange
Maldon sea salt flakes and freshly ground
black pepper
4 large slices of sourdough bread
4 figs, each cut into 5–6 segments

Heat a large frying pan over high heat. Line a plate with a double layer of paper towels.

When the frying pan is hot, add the bacon and fry for a few minutes on each side, until the fat has rendered and the bacon is golden brown, completely crisp, and can be crumbled with ease. Transfer to the paper towel–lined plate to drain the excess oil. When dry, crumble the bacon into a small bowl and crush it finely with a fork. Mix in the pul biber and honey and set aside.

Put the ricotta, dried thyme, and orange zest into a large bowl, season generously with salt and pepper, and whip until smooth and a little aerated.

Toast the bread, then divide the ricotta mixture among the slices. Reserve a little of the bacon mixture for sprinkling, then divide the remaining mixture into 4 portions and spoon 1 portion over the ricotta on each slice of bread. Arrange the fig segments on top, then sprinkle over the reserved bacon and a little dried thyme and pul biber to serve.

CARAMELIZED BANANA CRÊPES

with pistachios & honey

MAKES 12

¾ cup all-purpose flour, sifted

pinch of salt

2 eggs

¾ cup plus 1 tablespoon milk

¼ cup water

4 tablespoons salted butter, melted, plus an additional 6 tablespoons

1 heaping tablespoon superfine sugar

FOR THE TOPPING

3–4 tablespoons superfine sugar

3 large or 4 small bananas, peeled and sliced on the diagonal into 1-inch-thick slices

4 tablespoons salted butter

¾ cup pistachio nuts, roughly chopped

honey

To make the crêpe batter, put the flour, salt, and eggs in a large mixing bowl. Combine the milk and water in a small pitcher, then blend the liquid into the flour mixture a little at a time, mixing well with either a fork or an electric mixer to beat out any lumps. Mix in 2 tablespoons of melted butter and the sugar, then transfer the mixture to a measuring pitcher and set aside.

Set a heatproof plate over a pan of simmering water—you can keep the cooked crêpes warm by stacking them on this plate .

Heat a 7-inch frying pan over medium-high heat. Drizzle in 1 teaspoon of the melted butter and tilt the pan to spread it around the base of the pan. Quickly pour in just enough crêpe batter to barely coat the base (you want a nice, thin crêpe, not a pancake) and tilt the pan to spread the batter evenly. Cook until the edges start to curl up, about 1 minute, then use a knife to tease the edge of the crêpes over to check if the underside is golden and, if so, flip the crêpe (use a spatula if you like) and cook until the underside is golden brown, a further 30 seconds or so. Transfer the crêpe to the warm plate and cover with parchment paper. Repeat with the remaining batter, adding 1 teaspoon melted butter to the pan each time. Keep the crêpes warm while you cook the topping.

Put the superfine sugar in a shallow dish. Dip the 2 cut sides of each banana slice into the sugar to coat.

Put 2 tablespoons of the butter into a large frying pan set over high heat. Add half the banana slices and fry until slightly caramelized, or no more than 1 minute on each side. Remove from the pan and repeat with the remaining 2 tablespoons butter and banana slices.

To serve, place a few banana slices across half of each crêpe. Scatter over the pistachios and drizzle a little honey over each. Fold into quarters and serve immediately.

SPICED CHAI-FROSTED CUPCAKES

MAKES 12

FOR THE CUPCAKES

3 aromatic tea bags such as Earl Grey, Darjeeling, or English Breakfast

4 tablespoons boiling water

¾ cup milk

2 large eggs

5 tablespoons unsalted butter, softened

1¼ cups superfine sugar

1¾ cups all-purpose flour

1 tablespoon baking powder

1 heaping teaspoon ground cinnamon

1 heaping teaspoon ground ginger

good pinch of salt

FOR THE FROSTING

¼ cup milk

pinch of ground cloves

seeds from 4 cardamom pods, finely ground using a mortar and pestle

1 teaspoon ground cinnamon

4¼ cups confectioners' sugar

⅔ cup unsalted butter, softened

2 tablespoons dried edible rose petals, finely ground to a powder using a mortar and pestle or spice grinder

Put the tea bags in a bowl, add the 4 tablespoons of boiling water, and set aside to infuse for 30 minutes.

Preheat the oven to 375°F. Line a 12-cup muffin pan with paper liners.

In a measuring pitcher, whisk the milk and eggs together, then pour in the infused tea. Squeeze out every last drop of tea from the tea bags without bursting them. Place the used tea bags in a small bowl with the milk for the frosting, ground cloves, cardamom, and cinnamon and set aside to steep for at least 1 hour.

Put the butter, sugar, flour, baking powder, cinnamon, ginger, and salt in a large mixing bowl and combine slowly using an electric mixer on low speed until the mixture is evenly mixed.

Pour half the milk, egg, and tea mixture into the cake mixture and continue to blend on low speed, then increase the speed and mix until the mixture becomes nice and thick. Add the remaining milk, egg, and tea mixture and mix until smooth.

Divide the cake mixture among the lined muffin cups, filling them to within ½ inch from the top of the liners. Bake until nicely risen, about 20 minutes. Leave to cool in the pan for a few minutes, then transfer to a wire rack and leave to cool completely.

To make the frosting, remove the tea bags from the spiced milk mixture. Squeeze to extract all the flavor from the tea bags, then discard.

Put the confectioners' sugar, and butter in a mixing bowl. Using an electric mixer on low speed, combine until smooth, then add the spiced milk and continue to mix, increasing the speed gradually, until the frosting is light and creamy.

Frost the cooled cakes by swirling the frosting with a small palette knife, then sprinkle each with rose petal powder.

WEEKEND
FEASTS

I think many of us often spend the whole week looking forward to the weekend, only to reach the weekend and find its appeal wears off because we end up stuck in the kitchen for most of it. There are ways to enjoy your time in the kitchen without having to spend the entire weekend slaving away.

While it's always nice to whip up a feast midweek, sometimes, between the constraints of work and family life, it can all get a bit much. It's on the weekends that some of my best cooking is done. I find the relaxed, unhurried pace allows me to put a little more thought into the dish I'm preparing, and I get a lot more joy out of what I serve.

Many of us meet friends and family over the weekend, and sometimes—if you don't plan things carefully—you can end up regretting the decision to play host. And more importantly, you can easily miss out on valuable downtime spent enjoying the fruits of your labor. I realize that you may not want to spend a whole day cooking, but you still want to serve satisfying and impressive meals. With that in mind, I've put together this chapter of recipes that come together easily and that—with a little planning—enable you to enjoy more time around the table and less time toiling away in the kitchen. Some of the recipes can be scaled up to feed surprise visitors, so you can turn out weekend food that is delicious and perfect for sharing.

WEEKEND FEASTS

MENU

Chicken, pistachio & black pepper curry (page 42)

Cilantro, lime & garlic rice (page 49)

Pomegranate & eggplant salad with harissa & sun-dried tomatoes (page 52)

Tomato & olive salad with za'atar & a buttermilk dressing (page 57)

Peach, lime & pistachio polenta cake (page 63)

Accompaniment:
Mint tea mojitos (page 64)

CHICKEN, PISTACHIO &
BLACK PEPPER CURRY

SERVES 6

2 tablespoons vegetable oil

2 onions, roughly chopped

1¾ lb boneless, skinless chicken thighs

2 tablespoons coarse black pepper

a large bunch (about 1¾ oz) fresh cilantro, roughly chopped, plus additional leaves to garnish

seeds from 6 green cardamom pods

2 long red chiles

3-inch piece fresh ginger, peeled and roughly chopped

5 fat garlic cloves

¾ cups pistachio nuts

¾ lb peeled and deseeded butternut squash, cut into 2-inch-long, 1-inch-thick chunks

⅓ lb baby sweet corn

Maldon sea salt flakes

rice or naan, to serve

Heat the oil in a large saucepan over medium-high heat. Add the onions and fry until translucent and the edges start to brown, 6–8 minutes. Add the chicken and black pepper and seal the chicken by cooking for about 1 minute on all exposed sides, taking care not to let the chicken brown.

Put the cilantro, cardamom seeds, chiles, ginger, garlic, and pistachios in a blender with enough water to cover them all. Blend until the mixture is evenly green and silky-smooth with no lumps.

When the chicken is sealed, stir it well, then stir in the pistachio curry paste. Pour in just enough cold water to cover the chicken and paste mixture. Season generously with salt, and cook over low heat for 1 hour.

Check the seasoning and add more salt if needed, then stir in the butternut squash and baby sweet corn. Raise the heat to medium and cook for a further 30 minutes, or until the butternut squash and corn are both cooked and soft. Garnish with cilantro leaves and serve with rice or toasted naan bread.

TIP

You can also use bone-in chicken thighs — discard the skin and add an additional 30 minutes to the cooking time before adding the vegetables.

SAVORY PORK
& FENNEL BAKLAVA

with roasted tomatoes & feta

MAKES 9 SQUARES

2 lb pork shoulder or 2½-lb bone-in pork
    shoulder (leftover roast pork, lamb, or
    chicken also works well)

Maldon sea salt flakes and freshly ground
    black pepper

2¼ cups cherry tomatoes, halved

2 tablespoons fennel seeds

olive oil

1 large onion, thinly sliced into half-moons

2 fat garlic cloves, crushed

1⅔ cups passata

4 tablespoons honey

5 tablespoons unsalted butter, melted

6 sheets of filo pastry

8 oz feta cheese, crumbled

1 tablespoon nigella seeds, to garnish

FOR THE SYRUP

¾ cup boiling water

1½ cups superfine sugar

zest of 1 unwaxed orange

good pinch of cayenne pepper (optional)

Preheat the oven to 325°F. Place racks in the upper and lower thirds of the oven.

Put the pork into a roasting pan. Season the pork all over with a generous amount of salt and black pepper. Put the pork in the oven on the upper rack and roast for 3½–4 hours, covering the meat with aluminum foil for the final hour of cooking. Leave to cool in the pan.

Meanwhile, line a baking sheet with parchment paper or a silicone baking mat. Put the cherry tomato halves with their cut sides facing up on the prepared sheet. Roast the tomatoes on the lower rack, under the pork, until nicely burnished around the edges, about 1¾ hours. Leave to cool on the baking sheet.

Pick all the meat from the cooled pork and discard the fat and any skin. Shred the meat lightly with a knife and set aside.

Heat a large frying pan over medium-high heat, add the fennel seeds and toast, shaking the pan until they release their aroma and begin to brown a little, about 1 minute, taking care not to let them burn. Add a generous drizzle of olive oil, then add the onions and fry until translucent and the edges start to brown, 5–6 minutes. Stir in the garlic and shredded pork, then the passata, honey, and a generous amount of salt and pepper. Stir well, reduce the heat to medium-low and simmer gently for a few minutes, or until the sauce has reduced to a gravy-like consistency. Do not allow the sauce to become too dry—you want it to have a bit of moisture for a baklava. Remove the pan from the heat and leave to cool until the mixture is just warm.

Preheat the oven to 400°F. Brush the base of a 10- or 12-inch-square cake pan or ovenproof dish generously with some of the melted butter.

Line the base of the prepared pan with 4 sheets of filo pastry—2 lengthwise, 2 crosswise—allowing an equal amount of pastry to overhang each side of the pan. Brush the pastry with some of the melted butter. Spoon half the pork mixture into the pan and spread it evenly across the pastry. Scatter over half the cherry tomatoes and half of the crumbled feta. Fold 1 of the remaining pastry sheets to make a rough square shape and use to cover the layer of filling. Brush the pastry layer with some of the melted butter. Now repeat the process using the remaining pork mixture, tomatoes, and feta.

Fold over the overhanging pastry and brush with melted butter. Take the remaining pastry sheet, fold it into a square shape slightly larger than the surface and cover the top. Tuck the pastry edges down the sides of the pan using a round-bladed knife or similar, then brush the top liberally with the remaining melted butter. Using a very sharp knife, cut the top layers of pastry as neatly as possible either into 9 squares or, by cutting in diagonal lines, into diamond shapes (do this now, as it will be impossible to cut neatly after cooking). Bake until deep golden brown, about 30 minutes.

Meanwhile, make the syrup. Put the ¾ cup of boiling water into a small saucepan set over medium-high heat, then add the superfine sugar and dissolve it in the hot water. Add the orange zest and cayenne pepper, if using, stir well, then simmer gently until the mixture reduces to a syrup and can coat the back of a spoon, 10–15 minutes.

When the baklava is cooked, remove it from the oven and immediately pour the syrup evenly over the top, then scatter over the nigella seeds to garnish. Leave for 15 minutes to absorb the syrup before serving. To serve, either remove the whole baklava from the pan using a fish knife, transfer to a serving platter, and cut it at the table, or cut individual portions straight from the pan and serve with a green salad.

PAN-FRIED LAMB STEAKS, PRESERVED LEMON, CILANTRO & GARLIC

SERVES 4–6

FOR THE MARINADE

4 fat garlic cloves, crushed and thinly sliced

a small bunch (about 1 oz) fresh cilantro, finely chopped

6 preserved lemons, deseeded and finely chopped

1 tablespoon coarse black pepper

Maldon sea salt flakes

4–5 tablespoons olive oil

6–8 thin-cut lamb leg steaks (about ¼ lb each)

Put the garlic, cilantro, preserved lemons, and black pepper into a small bowl and season with just a little salt (as the preserved lemons are quite salty). Add the oil and mix well.

Put the lamb steaks in a large lock-top plastic bag and pour the marinade into the bag (or divide the lamb between 2 small lock-top plastic bags and add half the marinade to each bag). Seal the bag, then use your hands to work the marinade into the meat. Marinate at room temperature for a minimum of 20 minutes (although you can do this for a few hours in the refrigerator, too).

Set a large frying pan over medium-high heat. When hot, add the steaks and fry for about 6 minutes on each side, ensuring they are nicely coated with a little of the marinade. Leave to rest for a few minutes before serving. This should give you beautifully cooked pink lamb steaks.

CILANTRO, LIME & GARLIC RICE

SERVES 4–6

a large bunch (about 1¾ oz) fresh cilantro, roughly chopped

6 fat garlic cloves, crushed

6 large lime leaves, cut into strips

finely grated zest and juice of 1 unwaxed lime

3¼ cups cold water

2 heaping teaspoons coriander seeds

2 heaping teaspoons mustard seeds

olive oil

2¼ cups basmati rice

5 tablespoons unsalted butter

Maldon sea salt flakes

In a blender, blitz the fresh cilantro, garlic, lime leaves, and lime zest and juice together with 1 cup of the water. Once blended, stir in the remaining water and set aside.

Heat a large frying pan over medium-high heat, add the coriander and mustard seeds and toast, shaking the pan until they release their aroma and begin to brown a little, about 1 minute, taking care not to let them burn. Drizzle a little olive oil into the saucepan and stir in the rice, coating it well with the oil and spices. Add the butter. When melted, pour in the herb liquid, season generously with salt flakes, stir, and cover the pan with a lid. Simmer until the liquid has been absorbed, 20–25 minutes. Fluff the rice with a fork before serving.

SPICED GARLIC
SAVOY CABBAGE RIBBONS

SERVES 4–6

1 large head of savoy cabbage (or your favorite green, leafy cabbage), halved, core removed and leaves cut into 1-inch-thick ribbons

2 teaspoons cumin seeds

2 teaspoons coriander seeds

2 teaspoons mustard seeds

2 teaspoons nigella seeds

1–2 teaspoons red pepper flakes, to taste

olive oil

1 whole head of garlic, cloves crushed and thinly sliced

Maldon sea salt flakes and freshly ground black pepper

3 tablespoons unsalted butter, cut into cubes

6 tablespoons Greek yogurt

Wash and drain the cabbage ribbons, but do not shake off all the water as it will help to steam the cabbage later on.

Heat a large frying pan over medium-high heat, add the spices and toast, shaking the pan until they release their aroma and begin to brown a little, about 1 minute, taking care not to let them burn.

Drizzle in just enough olive oil to coat the base of the pan. Add the garlic and sauté for 1 minute, then pack half of the cabbage into the pan. Season this layer with a little salt and pepper and stir well. Add the remaining cabbage, season this top layer with salt and pepper, then add a little drizzle of oil. Cover the pan with a lid and cook for 3–4 minutes without removing the lid—instead, hold the lid on firmly and shake the pan to move the cabbage around and prevent it from sticking. This enables the cabbage to fry and steam at the same time.

Remove the lid and stir the cabbage well, ensuring the spices coat the cabbage, then add the butter and stir. Check and adjust the seasoning, then remove the pan from the heat. Stir in the yogurt and serve immediately.

POMEGRANATE & EGGPLANT SALAD

with harissa & sun-dried tomatoes

1–1¼ cups vegetable oil

2–3 large or 5 small eggplants, cut into 2-inch chunks

2 tablespoons olive oil

10 tablespoons pomegranate molasses

1 heaping tablespoon rose harissa

2–3 tablespoons honey, plus more to taste

2 heaping tablespoons tomato paste

2 slices of day-old sourdough bread (if using fresh, briefly toast and leave to dry for 1 hour), cut into cubes

⅓ lb sun-dried tomatoes in oil, drained and cut crosswise into strips

1 small bunch (about 1 oz) flat-leaf parsley, finely chopped

1¼ cups pomegranate seeds

¾ cup pistachio nuts

Maldon sea salt flakes

Pour the vegetable oil into a large, deep saucepan and heat over medium-high heat. Line a plate with a double layer of paper towels. Add the eggplant to the hot oil in the pan and fry until fully cooked and deeply golden brown on all sides, 10–15 minutes, stirring every few minutes to prevent burning. Remember that eggplant needs plenty of oil to cook properly, so add more oil if the pan becomes dry. Using a metal slotted spoon, transfer the cooked eggplant pieces to the paper towel–lined plate. Place two paper towels on top and press the eggplant pieces gently with the paper towels to extract the excess oil. Leave to cool.

Put the olive oil into a large mixing bowl with the pomegranate molasses, harissa, honey, and tomato paste and mix well. Add the stale bread cubes and coat them well with the mixture. Add the cooled eggplant, sun-dried tomatoes, parsley, pomegranate seeds, and pistachios and season well with salt. Mix thoroughly. At this point, you can add more honey to balance out the sour notes to your taste. Cover the bowl with plastic wrap and leave the salad to stand at room temperature for 30 minutes. The salad can also be made the day before and refrigerated overnight. Stir well before serving.

TIP

Don't be afraid about using this amount of oil to cook the eggplants—the excess oil can be squeezed out after cooking. To serve this as bruschetta, simply omit the bread from the recipe and serve on slices of toasted sourdough.

CELERIAC, ORANGE & CARAWAY SALAD

with a mustard yogurt dressing

SERVES 6–8

1 small celeriac or ½ very large one (exact quantity does not matter)

1 small bunch (about 1 oz) flat-leaf parsley, roughly chopped

2 teaspoons caraway seeds

½–¾ cup Greek yogurt (depending on the quantity of celeriac)

2 heaping tablespoons Dijon mustard (with or without seeds)

1 tablespoon olive oil

2 unwaxed oranges

Maldon sea salt flakes and freshly ground black pepper

Peel the celeriac and cut it into manageable chunks (3 usually works). Either grate them using the coarse holes of a box grater or shred them in a food processor using the shredding plate. Transfer to a mixing bowl. Reserve some of the chopped parsley for the garnish. Add the remaining chopped parsley, the caraway seeds, yogurt, mustard, and olive oil to the bowl and stir well until evenly combined. Finely grate the zest of the oranges directly into the bowl and mix again. Season with salt and pepper to taste.

To peel the zested oranges, use a small, sharp knife to cut away the top and bottom of the fruit. Rest the orange on the cut surface, then slice away strips of peel and pith to expose the flesh all around the orange. Halve each orange across the middle and cut into half-moons, then halve those half-moons. Add the orange pieces to the celeriac and fold them in gently so as not to crush them. Serve immediately scattered with the reserved chopped parsley.

TOMATO & OLIVE SALAD

with za'atar & a buttermilk dressing

SERVES 6–8

1¾ lb mixed tomatoes (any colors and
varieties you can find)

2 cups pitted mixed olives or 2½ cups if not
pitted (I like using Kalamata or a nice
firm green olive like Halkidiki)

¼ cup chives, snipped

Maldon sea salt flakes and freshly ground
black pepper

1 cup buttermilk

olive oil (try a flavored oil such as garlic
or lemon oil)

2 tablespoons za'atar

Slice the tomatoes horizontally into ½-inch-thick slices and arrange them on a large platter. Dot the platter with olives and scatter over half the snipped chives. Season generously with salt and pepper.

Season the buttermilk well with salt and a good slug of olive oil, then drizzle the buttermilk dressing over the salad. Scatter over the remaining chives and sprinkle over the za'atar. Serve immediately.

PRESERVED PEPPERS

stuffed with goat cheese & pine nuts

14-oz jar piquant preserved or brined
   whole mini red peppers (I use Peppadew)

10–15 oz soft goat cheese

finely grated zest of 2 unwaxed lemons

1 heaping teaspoon dried mint

1 small bunch (about 1 oz) mint, leaves
   finely chopped

½ cup toasted pine nuts, roughly chopped

freshly ground black pepper

Drain the peppers carefully and pat them dry with paper towels.

Put the goat cheese, lemon zest, dried and fresh mint, and pine nuts into a bowl, season generously with black pepper, and mix with a fork until evenly combined.

The fastest way to fill the peppers with the mixture is to use a piping bag fitted with a wide tip and pipe the mixture into each pepper. However, I confess I usually just fill the peppers carefully using a teaspoon and wipe off any smudges of cheese from each pepper with paper towels.

Serve the stuffed peppers immediately or refrigerate until ready to serve later in the day, or even the following day.

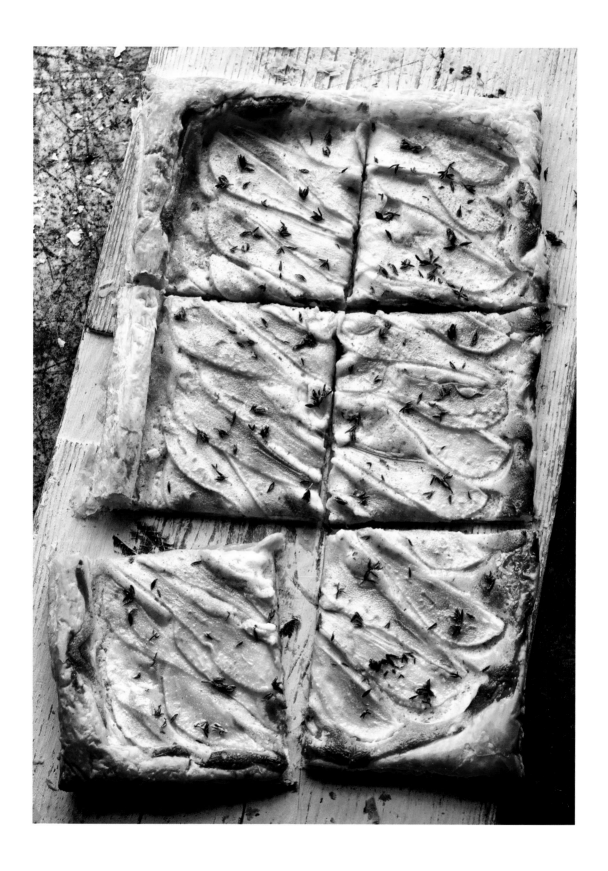

PEAR & THYME TART

SERVES 6–8

FOR THE CUSTARD

¾ cup heavy cream

2 egg yolks

1½ teaspoons vanilla bean paste

2 tablespoons thick strained Greek yogurt

1 tablespoon all-purpose flour

1 heaping tablespoon fresh thyme leaves, roughly chopped

2 tablespoons superfine sugar

1 sheet of frozen all-butter puff pastry, thawed

2 large Conference pears, peeled, halved, cored, and thinly sliced

small handful fresh thyme leaves

2 heaping tablespoons superfine sugar

½ teaspoon ground cinnamon

Preheat the oven to 400°F. Line a baking sheet with parchment paper.

To make the custard, combine the cream, egg yolks, vanilla bean paste, yogurt, and flour in a bowl and lightly beat with a whisk until it is evenly whipped and is the consistency of smooth, thick yogurt.

Using a mortar and pestle, pound the roughly chopped thyme leaves with the sugar until you have a smooth, thyme-infused sugar. Add the sugar to the custard mix and stir in until the mixture is very smooth and evenly combined.

Lay the unrolled puff pastry sheet in the prepared baking sheet. Score a 1-inch border around the edge of the pastry sheet and pour the custard mixture into the center. Carefully spread it out to the edge of the scored border. Lay the pear slices, diagonally overlapping each other, over the custard to cover it. Scatter over the thyme leaves and also the superfine sugar, then top with a scant sprinkle of cinnamon. Bake until the pastry edges are nicely browned, 25–28 minutes. Leave to cool before serving.

PEACH, LIME & PISTACHIO POLENTA CAKE

SERVES 8–10

3 peaches

3 large eggs

1 cup superfine sugar

3 unwaxed limes

⅔ cup fine polenta

1½ cups pistachio nuts, finely blitzed in a food processor or mini chopper

⅔ cup salted butter, melted and cooled slightly, plus more for greasing

FOR THE TOPPING

¾ cup Greek yogurt

1 peach

¼ cup pistachio nuts, roughly chopped

2 tablespoons honey

Put the 3 peaches into a small saucepan, cover with boiling water, and simmer until soft, about 25 minutes. Drain, then immediately plunge the peaches into cold water to cool them. Remove the pits, drain any excess water, then blitz the flesh in a blender until smooth.

Preheat the oven to 350°F. Grease a 9-inch springform cake pan and line it with parchment paper.

Beat the eggs and sugar together in a bowl. Finely grate the zest of 2½ of the limes directly into the bowl. Add the polenta and blitzed pistachios, then mix well. Stir in the cooled melted butter and, last, the peach purée. Pour the mixture into the prepared cake pan and bake until a toothpick inserted into the center of the cake comes out clean, 45–50 minutes. Leave the cake to cool completely in the pan or overnight.

Remove the cake from the pan and place it on a serving plate. Prepare the topping just before you are ready to serve. Spread the Greek yogurt straight from the refrigerator over the surface of the cake. Alternatively, if you're not going to eat the whole cake in one sitting, you can slice the cake into portions and top each slice individually (see Tip).

Slice the peach and arrange on top of the yogurt. Scatter over the pistachios and finely grate the zest of the remaining lime half over the top. Drizzle over the honey and serve immediately.

TIP

Leftover cake refrigerates incredibly well covered in plastic wrap, but bring it to room temperature to serve. You can always add the yogurt and topping to individual slices just before serving.

MINT TEA MOJITO

1 large bunch (about 1¾ oz) mint

8 teaspoons light brown sugar

1 cup boiling water

2 English Breakfast tea bags

4 unwaxed limes, halved and each half cut into 6 segments

1 cup dark rum

ice cubes

Pick 6 large mint leaves per glass and put them into 4 tumblers or highball glasses. Add 2 teaspoons of the sugar to each glass.

Pour the 1 cup of boiling water into a teapot or heatproof pitcher. Add mint sprigs and the tea bags and infuse for 3–4 minutes. Stir well and remove the tea bags but leave the mint in. Leave to cool.

Distribute the lime segments among the glasses. Using either a mojito muddler or the end of a wooden-spoon handle, crush the mint leaves, sugar, and lime pieces in each glass, extracting as much juice from the limes as possible. Pour ¼ cup of the dark rum into each glass.

If the mint tea is cool (throw a few ice cubes in to cool it if necessary), add ¼ cup of the tea to each glass. Add ice cubes and stir, then serve.

QUICK-FIX
FEASTS

I'm fairly certain when it comes to cooking a midweek dinner that the same thought often crosses our minds: "Should I cook tonight? Or would it be easier to just order a to-go meal?" I used to ask myself this question, and then I started to think "Okay, so if I order something to go, it takes 45 minutes, there are two of us, and there is no way it's coming in at less than $40, and it might not even be that great."

The truth is that sometimes we've just had a hectic day and are just too hard-pressed to cook a decent meal, and so convenience kicks in, whether store-bought or dialled for … and that's okay, because that's real life. But to those of you who don't believe it's possible to make something delicious in a short amount of time, using few ingredients, I want to say that it is possible. I promise you, this is how I cook virtually all the time at home.

Once in a while, I may make a labor-intensive recipe, if I know the results are truly worth it, but for an average, everyday midweek dinner, I know that if I have a few basic ingredients (let's say, a bit of cheese in the fridge, some vegetables or cupboard staples like pasta, beans or rice, combined with stuff from my spice rack and, if I'm lucky, some element of fresh produce—whether meat, dairy, vegetables or fruit), I can whip up something perfectly decent. And not only can I do this in less time than it takes to get something to go, but the chances are that it will taste better and be more satisfying.

In this chapter I have put together some of my favorite dishes for quick-turnaround meals, and I have also included a few side dishes that would suitably accompany any meal when you might need an additional element to bulk out a midweek feast. There is lots of flavor in these dishes but, in essence, the recipes are simple. Some are lighter, some need no cooking, and some are a complete meal all-in-one, but all are delicious and genuinely useful for those times when life takes over and you just want to cook, eat, and relax as quickly as possible.

QUICK-FIX FEASTS

MENU

Roasted cod fillets with wild thyme & pul biber (page 76)

Cumin-fried Padrón peppers with sumac, lemon & bread crumbs (page 85)

Burrata & burnt oranges with pistachios, mint & pomegranate (page 87)

Spicy halloumi salad with tomatoes & fried bread (page 88)

Accompaniment:
Toasted pita bread

ULTIMATE CHICKEN SHAWARMAS

SERVES 2-8

1¼ lb boneless, skinless chicken thigh
  fillets

1 teaspoon ground turmeric

1 teaspoon ground cinnamon

1 teaspoon ground coriander

1 teaspoon ground cumin

1 teaspoon cayenne pepper

4 fat garlic cloves, crushed

finely grated zest of 1 unwaxed lemon

juice of ½ lemon

4 tablespoons Greek yogurt

olive oil

Maldon sea salt flakes and freshly ground
  black pepper

TO SERVE

6-8 round flatbreads of your choosing
  (or use pitas)

¾ cup Greek yogurt

4 large tomatoes, sliced, then each slice
  cut in half

1 large red onion, halved and finely sliced
  into half-moons

1 small bunch (about 1 oz) fresh cilantro,
  roughly chopped

gherkins or cucumbers in brine (as many as
  you like), finely sliced

Place the chicken thigh fillets in a bowl. Add the spices, garlic, lemon zest and juice, yogurt, a good drizzle of olive oil (about 2 tablespoons), and a generous amount of salt and black pepper. Using your hands, work the marinade into the chicken, ensuring it is mixed evenly and coats every exposed part of all the fillets. Cover the bowl with plastic wrap and marinate for at least 30 minutes or overnight in the refrigerator.

Drizzle a little olive oil into a large frying pan set over medium heat. When the oil is hot, add the chicken—reduce the heat if the thighs begin to cook too quickly. Fry gently until the thighs have a nice, deep golden-brown crust and are cooked through, 10–12 minutes on each side. When done, remove and cut the thighs crosswise very thinly.

To serve, lay a flatbread on your work surface. Spread Greek yogurt across the surface. Place a line of tomato half-moons down the middle. Stack some shredded chicken over the tomatoes, then follow with the onion, cilantro, and a few slices of pickled cucumbers. Fold up the bottom of the flatbread, then fold over the sides to enclose the filling as tightly as possible. Repeat with the remaining flatbreads and filling. To make eating the shawarmas a little easier, and to hold the juices in, wrap the base with some doubled-up waxed or parchment paper, or a square of aluminum foil.

HARISSA SKIRT STEAK SANDWICHES

with sweet red onion pickle

2 lb skirt steaks

4 tablespoons rose harissa

vegetable oil

1–2 baguettes (depending on how much bread you like)

Maldon sea salt flakes and freshly ground black pepper

2 handfuls mixed salad leaves

FOR THE SWEET RED ONION PICKLE

2 red onions, halved and thinly sliced into half-moons

4 tablespoons rice wine vinegar (or use red or white wine vinegar)

2 teaspoons pul biber chile flakes

2 teaspoons nigella seeds

½ small bunch (about ½ oz) dill, roughly chopped

3 tablespoons superfine sugar

Coat the steaks well in the rose harissa, using your hands to really work the spice into the meat. When evenly coated on both sides, lay out the steaks, stacked on top of each other, on a plate and cover with plastic wrap. Leave to marinate for 20 minutes.

Combine all the ingredients for the onion pickle in a bowl and mix well, ensuring the pickle dressing has evenly coated all the onions. Set aside.

Drizzle a little oil into a large, heavy-bottomed frying pan and set it over medium-high heat. When the oil is hot, place as much steak into the pan as you can cook in one go without overcrowding. Cook according to your liking—the length of time depends on the thickness of the steak. The best way to check is to test its firmness by poking the fattest part with your finger; if it is still very bouncy, it will be very rare. The firmer it becomes, the more well done the meat is. Ideally, you want something lovely and pinkish red on the inside so the cut is at its peak—juicy, tender, and cooked to perfection. I find with most skirt steaks that 4–5 minutes cooking on each side over medium-high heat does the trick. Transfer the cooked steak to a plate, cover with aluminum foil, and leave to rest for 5 minutes as you continue cooking subsequent batches.

Once rested, slice the steak crosswise into thin, juicy slivers. Season well with salt and pepper. Pile the slices into as much or as little bread as you like. Stir the pickle once more, then serve with the pickle spooned over the meat and some mixed salad leaves on top.

ROASTED COD FILLETS

with wild thyme & pul biber

SERVES 4

4 cod fillets (about ½ lb each), thicker pieces work best

garlic oil

4 teaspoons dried wild thyme

2 teaspoons pul biber chile flakes

finely grated zest of 2 unwaxed lemons

Maldon sea salt flakes and freshly ground black pepper

Preheat the oven to 425°F. Line a roasting pan with parchment paper.

Place the fish fillets on the prepared roasting pan and drizzle generously with garlic oil to coat each piece of fish. Sprinkle over the wild thyme, pul biber, lemon zest, and a generous amount of salt and pepper.

Roast until the fish is cooked through, 8–12 minutes, depending on the thickness of your fish. Serve immediately.

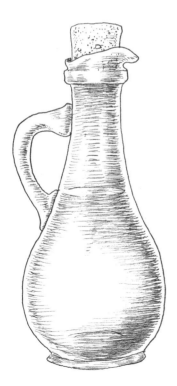

EASTERN SHRIMP LINGUINE

with feta, garlic, pul biber & Greek basil

SERVES 4–6

olive oil

6 fat garlic cloves, crushed and thinly sliced

1 lb linguine

1¼ lb raw, peeled shrimp

3 tablespoons unsalted butter

Maldon sea salt flakes and freshly ground black pepper

finely grated zest of 2 unwaxed lemons

2–3 tablespoons pul biber chile flakes

14 oz feta cheese, broken into rough ½-inch chunks

several handfuls Greek basil leaves

Drizzle a generous amount of oil into a large frying pan set over medium heat. When the oil is hot, add the garlic slices and cook until they are translucent and soft, about 2 minutes, taking care not to let them brown. Remove the pan from the heat and set it aside to allow the garlic to infuse the oil.

Cook the pasta according to the package instructions. Drain the pasta, reserving a couple of ladlefuls of the cooking water, and return the pasta to the pan.

Put the frying pan with the garlic back on the stove, add the shrimp, and fry them over medium-high heat until they are pink, opaque, and completely cooked through, a few minutes on each side.

Pour the contents of the frying pan into the cooked pasta. Add the butter and the reserved pasta cooking liquid and season generously with salt and pepper. Add the lemon zest and pul biber and stir well, then add the feta and Greek basil. Toss well and serve with an additional drizzle of olive oil.

CHICORY & PEAR SALAD

with sriracha honey dressing

SERVES 4–6

¾–1 lb chicory, leaves separated

2 pears (any variety), sliced into very
   fine disks

½ cup pistachio nuts

FOR THE DRESSING

4 tablespoons sriracha sauce

2 tablespoons honey, plus more to taste

juice of ½ lemon

2 tablespoons olive oil

Maldon sea salt flakes and freshly ground
   black pepper

Put the chicory leaves into a large bowl and add the pear slices
and pistachios.

Using a small whisk or fork, mix the dressing ingredients
together in a cup. Adjust the sweetness by adding more honey
if desired, then pour the dressing over the salad, toss well and
serve immediately.

BLACK-EYED PEA SALAD

with diced peppers, spring onions, dill & parsley

SERVES 4–6

2 cans (15 oz each) black-eyed peas

1 red pepper, cored, deseeded, and finely diced

1 green pepper, cored, deseeded, and
   finely diced

5 spring onions, thinly sliced from root to tip

1 small bunch (about 1 oz) dill, finely chopped

1 small bunch (about 1 oz) flat-leaf parsley,
   finely chopped

2 celery stalks, cut lengthwise into 3,
   then diced

3 tablespoons red wine vinegar

4 tablespoons olive oil

Maldon sea salt flakes and freshly ground
   black pepper

Combine all the ingredients in a large bowl and mix well.
Leave to rest for 20 minutes, then mix again, taste and adjust
the seasoning if desired, then serve.

SPICY CHICKPEA, HARISSA & CHEDDAR PITAS

MAKES 10

1 teaspoon cumin seeds

1 teaspoon coriander seeds

olive oil

1 onion, finely chopped

3 fat garlic cloves, crushed

1 can (15 oz) chickpeas, drained

1 teaspoon ground turmeric

½ teaspoon ground cinnamon

finely grated zest of 1 unwaxed lemon

juice of ½ lemon

Maldon sea salt flakes and freshly ground black pepper

1 small bunch (about 1 oz) fresh cilantro, finely chopped

TO SERVE

1 heaping tablespoon rose harissa

10 mini pita breads

5 oz mature Cheddar cheese, coarsely grated

Heat a large frying pan over medium-high heat, add the cumin and coriander seeds and toast until they release their aroma and begin to brown a little, about 1 minute, shaking the pan and taking care not to let them burn. Crush the toasted seeds with a mortar and pestle. Set aside.

Return the frying pan to the burner. Add a good drizzle of olive oil and the onion and fry until translucent and the edges start to brown, 6–8 minutes. Add the garlic, crushed cumin and coriander seeds, chickpeas, turmeric, and cinnamon and mix well. As you stir, lightly mash some (but not all) of the chickpeas to create texture. Now add the lemon zest and juice and season generously with salt and pepper. Mix well, then remove the pan from the heat. Stir in the cilantro, reserving a little to garnish, and set aside.

Put the rose harissa in a bowl and stir in a drizzle of olive oil to loosen the consistency a little.

Lightly toast the pitas, just to warm them through. Slice open each pita and spoon the chickpeas inside. Top with a little of the harissa mixture, some grated cheese, and a little of the reserved fresh cilantro to finish. Serve immediately.

CUMIN-FRIED PADRÓN PEPPERS

with sumac, lemon & bread crumbs

SERVES 4–6

2 tablespoons cumin seeds

garlic oil

¾ lb Padrón peppers

Maldon sea salt flakes

2 handfuls fine, dried, natural bread
  crumbs (not golden)

1 tablespoon sumac

finely grated zest of 1 unwaxed lemon

Heat a large frying pan or saucepan over high heat and have a lid or splatter guard at hand. Pour in the cumin seeds, then add a generous amount of garlic oil to coat the base of the pan. Follow immediately with the Padrón peppers and stir-fry for 2 minutes, ensuring they are coated in the cumin seeds and oil. Cover the pan with a lid—you will hear the cumin seeds pop. At this point, shake the pan gently to toss the peppers, holding the lid on tightly. The peppers will start to shrivel, and after about 1 minute the skins will brown and blister. When this happens, transfer the peppers to a board or serving platter and season with a generous amount of sea salt flakes (do not crush the flakes—just scatter them over).

Return the pan to the burner, add the bread crumbs and fry over medium-high heat until golden brown and crispy, 30–40 seconds. Scatter the bread crumbs over the peppers, followed by the sumac and lemon zest, then serve immediately.

BURRATA & BURNT ORANGES

with pistachios, mint & pomegranate

SERVES 2–4

1 orange or blood orange

extra-virgin olive oil

½ lb ball of burrata

⅓ cup pomegranate seeds

¼ cup pistachio nuts, roughly chopped

2 pinches of nigella seeds

½ teaspoon sumac

Maldon sea salt flakes and freshly ground black pepper

handful of mint leaves, torn

To segment the orange, use a small, sharp knife to cut away the top and bottom of the fruit. Rest the orange on the cut surface, then slice away strips of peel and pith to expose the flesh all around the orange. When peeled, slice out segments of orange and discard the leftover skin.

You can use one of two methods to burn the orange segments: either use a kitchen torch to blacken the slices on both sides or, alternatively, heat a frying pan on the highest heat available until hot, brush a little oil onto both sides of the segments, and place them in the pan. Leave them to cook until starting to blacken, about 1 minute on each side.

Place the ball of burrata in the center of a serving plate and either leave it whole or (if you're like me) pull it apart into rough quarters (roughly scoring the top makes this easier to do). Arrange the burnt orange segments on the plate and scatter over the pomegranate seeds, pistachios, nigella seeds, and sumac. Drizzle generously with olive oil, season with salt and pepper, scatter over the torn mint leaves and serve.

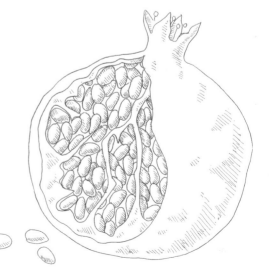

SPICY HALLOUMI SALAD

with tomatoes & fried bread

SERVES 4–6

1¼ lb tomatoes, cut into rough chunks

1 large red onion, finely sliced

1 large cucumber, halved lengthwise,
    halved again and cut into 1-inch dice

2 tablespoons dried oregano

finely grated zest and juice of 1 unwaxed
    lemon

olive oil

1 teaspoon Maldon sea salt flakes,
    plus more to season

freshly ground black pepper

2 heaping teaspoons cumin seeds

2 heaping teaspoons coriander seeds

2 teaspoons black mustard seeds

1 heaping teaspoon red pepper flakes,
    plus more to taste

garlic oil (optional)

4–5 thick slices of sourdough bread
    or similar, preferably stale or left out
    to dry, cubed

2 x ½-lb blocks of halloumi cheese,
    each cut into 5 slices

1 small bunch (about 1 oz) mint, leaves
    picked, rolled up tightly and cut into thin
    ribbons, to garnish

Put the tomatoes, onion, and cucumber chunks into a large mixing bowl. Add the oregano, lemon zest and juice, and a good drizzle of olive oil, season well with salt and pepper and mix well. Set aside.

Heat a large frying pan over medium-high heat, add the cumin seeds, coriander seeds, mustard seeds, and pepper flakes and toast until they release their aroma and begin to brown a little, about 1 minute, shaking the pan and taking care not to let them burn. Transfer to a mortar and add the 1 teaspoon sea salt flakes. Using a pestle, crush the seeds lightly to break them down just a little—you want to keep a lot of the texture. Add the crushed seed mix to the tomato salad and mix well.

Line a plate with a double layer of paper towels. Set the same frying pan in which you toasted the seeds over medium-high heat and drizzle in some olive or garlic oil. Once the oil is hot, add the bread cubes and fry on both sides until deep golden, 4–5 minutes. Transfer to the paper towel–lined plate and set aside.

Drizzle a little olive oil into the same pan, add the halloumi slices, and fry until golden brown, 1–2 minutes on each side.

Add the fried bread to the salad and toss well to coat the bread chunks in the dressing. Adjust the seasoning as necessary, then arrange the salad and halloumi on a large platter and sprinkle with mint ribbons just before serving.

ROASTED APRICOTS

with ricotta, honey & pistachio crunch

SERVES 6

2 handfuls fine, dried, natural bread crumbs (not golden)

½ cup pistachio nuts, blitzed in a food processor or mini chopper or finely chopped

6–9 apricots (1 large apricot or 1½ small apricots per serving)

freshly ground black pepper

½ lb ricotta cheese

honey, for drizzling

Preheat the oven to the very highest temperature. Line a baking sheet with parchment paper.

Heat a large frying pan over medium-high heat. Add the bread crumbs and toast for 6 minutes, then add the pistachios and fry until the mixture is crunchy and golden, 1–2 minutes. Remove from the heat and set aside.

Carefully halve and pit the apricots, then season with a good grinding of black pepper. Lay them on the prepared baking sheet with their cut sides facing upward. They do not need any oil or other fat. Roast the apricots until the edges are burnished and the fruit is slightly softened, about 10 minutes. Leave to cool.

Spoon a neat little spoonful or quenelle of ricotta on top of each apricot half, then drizzle over some honey. Scatter over the pistachio and bread crumb "crunch," then serve.

RASPBERRY, CARDAMOM & VANILLA YOGURT FOOL

SERVES 6–8

3¼ cups fresh raspberries

2 teaspoons vanilla bean paste

seeds from 5 cardamom pods, crushed
using a mortar and pestle

1¼ cups heavy cream

1–3 tablespoons confectioners' sugar
(depending on the sweetness of the fruit)

2 cups thick Greek yogurt

Reserve 6–8 of the raspberries for the garnish.

Using a food processor, blitz the remaining raspberries with the vanilla bean paste and crushed cardamom seeds until smooth.

Using an electric mixer, beat the heavy cream and confectioners' sugar together until stiff peaks form, then gently fold in the yogurt, one-third at a time. When all the yogurt is incorporated, gently fold in half the raspberry sauce, ensuring you fold (rather than stir) it in, to keep as much air in the mixture as possible. When incorporated, fold in the remaining raspberry sauce.

Divide the mixture among 6–8 glasses or dessert bowls. Place a raspberry on top of each serving. Refrigerate for at least 2 hours to firm up, or serve immediately if you can't wait.

TIP

I sometimes like to serve these with shortbread cookies on the side.

VEGETARIAN

FEASTS

The culinary world has evolved so much in the past 20 years that being vegetarian no longer means you need to suffer the limitations of bland, ill-thought-out dishes. And while many of us love a mushroom risotto or a nut roast, food has moved on. Personally, I've always felt the flavors and techniques of Middle Eastern cooking are incredibly well suited to vegetarians and vegans.

I have many vegetarian friends and can empathize with the lack of love that goes in to creating dishes to accommodate them at times. Since I became a chef and needed to create inspiring vegetarian dishes, I have embraced vegetables more than ever before. While I may not be a vegetarian, I have found that there are plenty of ways to create satisfying meals using vegetables that will please everyone around the table. A humble root vegetable can be brought to life with a little sprinkle of spice and just a couple more ingredients. Coming up with a vegetarian feast (not just a collection of recipes that feel like side dishes) can be easy if you combine a few straightforward ingredients from the kitchen cupboard with some fresh produce. You can create something not only abundant, colorful and simple but also—and most importantly—utterly satisfying.

More and more people are adding meat-free days to their weekly diets and there is absolutely no need for this to be a bland and tasteless affair. It's not complicated to create vegetarian dishes that will satisfy vegetarians and meat-eaters alike. For the carnivores among you, I am confident that you will find the following recipes in this chapter filling and satisfying (and likewise, vegetarians—there are plenty more meat-free recipes throughout this book) to keep your table filled with delicious dishes. And you don't need to label this as vegetarian cuisine because, really, it's just hearty, delicious, satisfying food. That's the best kind of food, I'm sure you'll agree.

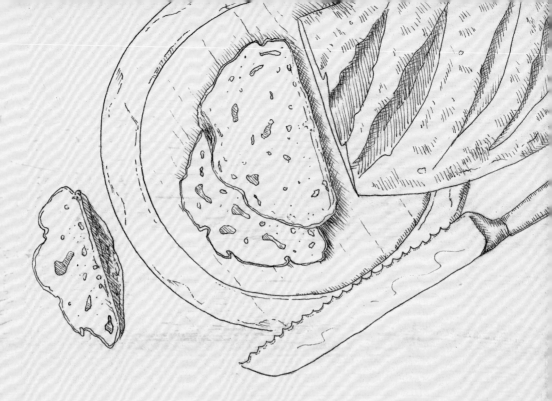

VEGETARIAN FEASTS

—

MENU

Polenta sticks with cumin, garlic & feta (page 100)

Quinoa patties with pomegranate molasses & yogurt (page 103)

Carrot, orange, ginger & walnut dip (page 104)

Green couscous & roasted vegetables with black garlic & preserved lemons (page 109)

Sticky, spicy eggplants with toasted sesame seeds & spring onions (page 110)

Spiced green bean & tomato stew with labneh, harissa oil & scorched peanuts (page 113)

Accompaniments:
Harissa yogurt; toasted ciabatta

POLENTA STICKS

with cumin, garlic & feta

MAKES 20

1 heaping teaspoon cumin seeds

1¼ cups polenta

4–5 fat garlic cloves, crushed

finely grated zest of 1 large unwaxed lime

Maldon sea salt flakes and freshly ground
   black pepper

2 cups boiling water

1 teaspoon red pepper flakes (optional)

1 small bunch (about 1 oz) fresh cilantro,
   finely chopped

8 oz feta cheese, crumbled

vegetable oil

2 eggs, beaten

Heat a large frying pan over medium-high heat, add the cumin seeds and toast, shaking the pan until they release their aroma and begin to brown a little, about 1 minute, taking care not to let them burn. Add ¾ cup of the polenta, the garlic, lime zest, salt, pepper, and the boiling water and stir vigorously to ensure the polenta breaks up and is a smooth, even consistency without lumps. Do not be tempted to add more water as this will make the sticks impossible to fry. Transfer the cooked polenta to a plate, spread it out, and leave to cool.

When cooled, put the cooked polenta into a mixing bowl and add the red pepper flakes, if using, cilantro, and crumbled feta. Mix well until the ingredients are evenly incorporated.

Lay a sheet of parchment paper on a baking sheet. Divide the mixture into 2 equal portions and spread out each portion into a long rectangular shape roughly 10 x 4 inches and about 1 inch thick. (Don't get too caught up with exact measurements— these are just a guideline.) Cut each block into 10 sticks, then put in the freezer for 1 hour to firm up.

Pour enough oil into a large saucepan or deep-frying pan to deep-fry the polenta sticks and heat over medium-high heat. Line a plate with a double layer of paper towels. Prepare 2 shallow dishes, one with the beaten eggs and one with the remaining polenta.

When the oil is hot, remove the polenta sticks from the freezer. Coat each stick all over, first in the egg, then in the polenta. Carefully lower the sticks into the hot oil and fry until crisp and golden, about 2 minutes on each side. Remove with a metal slotted spoon and transfer to the paper towel–lined plate to drain the excess oil, then serve.

QUINOA PATTIES

with pomegranate molasses & yogurt

MAKES 16–18

1⅛ cups quinoa

1 large egg

1 onion, very finely chopped

2 heaping teaspoons turmeric

2 heaping teaspoons ground cumin

1 heaping teaspoon ground cinnamon

¼ lb ready-to-eat dried apricots, finely chopped (raisins or dried cranberries also work well)

1 small bunch (about 1 oz) fresh cilantro, finely chopped

Maldon sea salt flakes and freshly ground black pepper

4 tablespoons vegetable oil, plus more if needed

TO SERVE

¾ cup Greek yogurt

Maldon sea salt flakes and freshly ground black pepper

½ cup pomegranate molasses

Cook the quinoa for a little longer than the package instructions (about 10–12 minutes), or until it is quite soft and swollen. Drain and rinse very well under cold running water to remove the starch and ensure all the quinoa is well rinsed and not stuck together. Shake well, then leave to drain.

Put the quinoa, egg, onion, spices, apricots, and chopped cilantro (reserving 1 tablespoon for garnish) into a large mixing bowl, season with salt and pepper, and stir together. Squeeze the mixture with your hands so it sticks together. Shape the mixture into golf ball–size balls, then pat them down to form nice, equal-size patties—don't worry about making them too perfect, but ensure they are no thicker than ¾ inch.

Heat the oil in a large frying pan over medium-high heat. Line a plate with a double layer of paper towels. Add the patties to the pan (in batches if necessary to avoid overcrowding the pan) and fry until deep golden brown, 4–5 minutes on each side. If necessary, add a little more oil as they cook in order to get a nice crunchy base on each patty. Transfer the cooked patties to the paper towel–lined plate and leave to drain any excess oil.

Put the yogurt into a pitcher and season with salt and pepper. Stir in just enough water to thin the yogurt to the consistency of heavy cream.

Serve the patties with a generous amount of seasoned yogurt drizzled over, followed by the pomegranate molasses and a scattering of the reserved fresh cilantro.

CARROT, ORANGE, GINGER & WALNUT DIP

SERVES 6-8

1 lb carrots, peeled and cut into 3 pieces

1½ cups whole shelled walnuts

1 small bunch (about 1 oz) fresh cilantro, finely chopped

1 heaping teaspoon ground cinnamon

½ teaspoon ground cloves

4-inch piece fresh ginger, peeled and finely grated

2-3 fat garlic cloves, crushed

2 tablespoons honey

zest and juice of 2 unwaxed oranges

extra-virgin olive oil

Maldon sea salt flakes and freshly ground black pepper

3 tablespoons nigella seeds

Cook the carrots in boiling water for 10 minutes, or until cooked through. Drain, then immediately plunge the carrots into cold water to stop the cooking process.

Using a food processor, combine the walnuts (reserving a few for garnish), carrots, cilantro (reserving some for garnish), spices, ginger, garlic, honey, and orange zest and juice along with a generous glug (about 4 tablespoons) of olive oil. Blitz the mixture to a coarsely textured purée. Season with salt and pepper to taste. Drizzle in a little more olive oil to loosen the consistency if desired. Last, stir through the nigella seeds and serve with the reserved cilantro and a few reserved walnut pieces arranged on top.

ROASTED PORTOBELLO MUSHROOMS

with pine nuts & halloumi

SERVES 4 AS A STARTER OR SIDE

4 large Portobello mushrooms

¼ cup unsalted butter, softened

2 fat garlic cloves, crushed

1 small bunch (about 1 oz) fresh cilantro, very finely chopped

4 oz halloumi cheese, coarsely grated

2-3 tablespoons pine nuts, finely chopped

Maldon sea salt flakes and freshly ground black pepper

olive oil

Preheat the oven to 425°F. Line a baking sheet with parchment paper.

Arrange the mushrooms on the prepared tray with their gills facing upward.

Combine the butter, garlic, cilantro, halloumi, and pine nuts in a bowl and season well. Drizzle in just a little olive oil and mix well. Divide the mixture into 4 portions and pile 1 portion into the center of each mushroom, pressing it into the base.

Roast until nicely browned, 35-40 minutes, then serve.

ROASTED BEET SALAD

with burnt chestnuts, tahini yogurt & herb oil

SERVES 4

3¼ lb beets, roasted and peeled (or use
vacuum-packed beets in natural juices),
quartered

½ lb vacuum-packed cooked and
peeled chestnuts

FOR THE HERB OIL
½ small bunch (about ½ oz) dill
½ small bunch (about ½ oz) fresh cilantro
a good squeeze of lemon juice
finely grated zest of 1 unwaxed lemon
5 tablespoons olive oil, plus more as needed
Maldon sea salt flakes and freshly ground
black pepper

FOR THE YOGURT SAUCE
3 tablespoons tahini
½ cup Greek-style yogurt
2–3 tablespoons olive oil
1–2 tablespoons warm water

TO GARNISH
toasted sesame seeds
toasted nigella seeds

Arrange the beet quarters on a large platter.

Heat a large saucepan over high heat. Put the chestnuts into
the pan without oil and scorch them a little, about 2 minutes
on each side, or until they are slightly blackened. Remove the
chestnuts from the heat and arrange them on the platter with
the beets.

To make the herb oil, pour a little boiling water into a bowl
and immerse the dill and cilantro in it. Leave to blanch
for 1 minute, then drain and cool the herbs under cold
running water.

Using a mini food processor, blitz the herbs with a squeeze of
lemon juice, the lemon zest, olive oil, and some salt and pepper.
Blend to a smooth mixture, adding more oil to loosen the
consistency as necessary. Adjust the seasoning to taste and
set aside.

In a bowl or measuring cup with a spout, combine the
ingredients for the yogurt sauce, adding just enough of the
warm water to give the mixture a smooth sauce consistency.
Drizzle the yogurt sauce over the beet. Spoon over the herb
oil, then sprinkle with toasted sesame seeds and nigella seeds
to garnish.

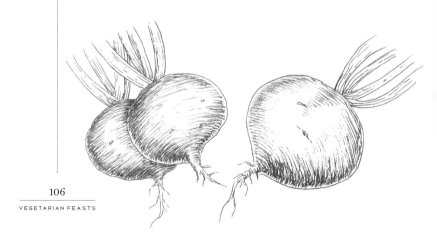

GREEN COUSCOUS
& ROASTED VEGETABLES

with black garlic & preserved lemons

2 zucchini, halved lengthwise and sliced into ½-inch-thick half moons

1 red pepper, cored, deseeded and cut into 1-inch squares

1 yellow or green pepper, cored, deseeded and cut into 1-inch squares

2 red onions, halved and sliced into ½-inch-thick half-moons

olive oil

Maldon sea salt flakes and freshly ground black pepper

10½ oz couscous

6–8 preserved lemons, thinly sliced into rounds

1 head of black garlic, cloves thinly sliced

FOR THE HERB OIL

1¾ oz flat-leaf parsley, leaves and stems roughly chopped

1 large bunch (about 1¾ oz) fresh cilantro, roughly chopped

olive oil

Preheat the oven to its highest temperature. Line a large baking sheet with parchment paper.

Put the zucchini, peppers, and onions on the baking sheet. Drizzle with a good amount of olive oil and season with salt and pepper. Use your hands to coat all the pieces in seasoned oil, then spread the pieces across the sheet. Roast until nicely brown, about 15 minutes, or as desired.

Prepare the couscous according to the package instructions, then fluff with a fork.

To prepare the herb oil, use a mini food processor or an immersion blender to blitz the parsley and cilantro with enough olive oil to give the mixture a smooth herb oil consistency (a few tablespoons will do the trick). Season heavily with salt (as this salt will season the entire quantity of couscous) and, using a fork, stir the herb oil through the couscous until it is evenly combined. Last, stir in the roasted vegetables, preserved lemons and black garlic. Serve hot or at room temperature.

STICKY, SPICY EGGPLANTS

with toasted sesame seeds & spring onions

SERVES 4–6 AS A SIDE

vegetable oil

3 large or 4 medium eggplants, halved lengthwise and cut into 1-inch-thick half-moons

about 2 heaping tablespoons rose harissa, plus more as desired

4 tablespoons honey, plus more as desired

Maldon sea salt flakes and freshly ground black pepper

TO GARNISH

2 teaspoons sesame seeds, lightly toasted

1 teaspoon nigella seeds

½ small bunch (about ½ oz) fresh cilantro, leaves roughly chopped

4 spring onions, thinly sliced from root to tip

Heat a large saucepan over high heat and add enough oil to fill ½ inch up the side. Line a plate with a double layer of paper towels. Add the eggplant to the pan and coat them in the hot oil. Eggplants are like sponges and will immediately absorb the oil but, once cooked through, they will release some oil again. Fry the eggplant until they begin to shrink, soften, and take on an even golden brown color on all sides, 10–12 minutes, adding more oil as necessary to help them cook and tossing them every few minutes. Using a metal slotted spoon, transfer to the paper towel–lined plate. Lay 2 paper towels over the eggplant pieces to absorb excess oil.

Use paper towels to wipe any remaining oil from the frying pan. Transfer the eggplant back into the pan and add the harissa, honey, and a generous amount of salt and pepper. Stir well until the eggplant pieces are evenly coated in the mixture. Taste and adjust the levels of honey, harissa, and seasoning as desired. Serve with the sesame seeds, nigella seeds, cilantro, and spring onions scattered over.

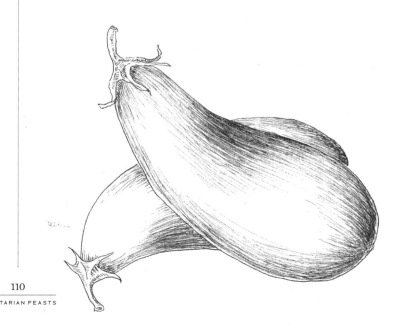

SPICED GREEN BEAN & TOMATO STEW

with labneh, harissa oil & scorched peanuts

SERVES 4–6

olive oil

1 large head of garlic, cloves bashed and
    thinly sliced

1 lb trimmed green beans

2 teaspoons ground cumin

1 heaping teaspoon ground cinnamon

1 heaping teaspoon ground turmeric

1 lb tomatoes, cored and diced into
    rough chunks

1 can (14½ oz) chopped tomatoes

1 heaping teaspoon superfine sugar

Maldon sea salt flakes and freshly ground
    black pepper

TO SERVE

1 heaping tablespoon rose harissa

olive oil

1 cup labneh

2 generous handfuls of peanuts,
    toasted until slightly scorched

Drizzle enough oil into a large saucepan to generously coat the base and heat over medium heat. Add the garlic slivers and stir-fry for 1–2 minutes, or until they soften. Add the green beans and cook until they just begin to lose their rawness, 4–5 minutes; they will deepen in color to a more vibrant green and soften somewhat.

Stir the spices and fresh tomatoes into the saucepan, then raise the heat and add the canned tomatoes, sugar, and a generous amount of salt and pepper. Simmer, stirring occasionally, until the beans are well cooked and the sauce has somewhat reduced, about 20 minutes. Taste and adjust the seasoning if desired.

Put the harissa into a small pitcher and mix in enough olive oil to thin it to a slightly runny consistency.

Serve warm on a platter or in a shallow bowl, dotted with dollops of labneh and harissa oil and scattered with the scorched peanuts.

GARLIC, FENUGREEK & CUMIN FLATBREADS

SERVES 6

2 cups whole-wheat flour, plus more
for dusting

2 large pinches of Maldon sea salt
flakes, crushed

1 teaspoon red pepper flakes (optional)

3 tablespoons dried fenugreek leaves

2 fat garlic cloves, crushed

olive oil or ghee

¾ cup lukewarm water, plus more
as needed

6 pinches (about 1½ teaspoons total)
cumin seeds

melted butter, to serve (optional)

Put the flour into a large mixing bowl and make a well in the center. Put the crushed salt, pepper flakes, if using, fenugreek, garlic, 1 tablespoon of the olive oil, and the lukewarm water into the well. Mix with a fork, incorporating the flour into the wet mixture, until a dough begins to form. If the mixture is too wet, add more flour to bring it together; if it is too dry, mix in a little more lukewarm water to bring the mixture to a good dough consistency. Knead for 5 minutes. Leave to rest for 10 minutes, then knead once again for 2 minutes.

Dust your work surface with flour. Divide the dough into 6 equal balls and roll out each ball into a rough circle. Sprinkle each with a pinch of cumin seeds and press them into the dough.

Fold the circles in half and in half again. Roll out the folded dough gently into 6-inch circles, applying very little pressure to your rolling pin—too much compression prevents the light layers from puffing up during cooking. Pour ½ teaspoon of the olive oil into a frying pan set over medium heat. When the oil is hot, fry 1 of the dough circles until the underside is golden in patches, about 1 minute, then turn it over and fry for a further 1 minute, or until golden.

Stack the cooked flatbreads between layers of parchment paper while you repeat with the remaining dough circles, using ½ teaspoon of oil each time to fry them. Serve brushed with melted butter or additional ghee if desired.

SPICED RHUBARB
& ALMOND CAKE

SERVES 8–10

1 lb rhubarb, trimmed and cut into
  ¼-inch-thick slices

1⅛ cups superfine sugar, plus
  2 tablespoons

3 teaspoons ground cinnamon

3 large eggs

2 teaspoons vanilla bean paste

2 teaspoons ground ginger

1¾ cups self-rising flour

⅔ cup salted butter, melted, plus more
  for greasing

1¾ cups sliced almonds, ¾ cup toasted

FOR THE FILLING

1¼ cups heavy cream, cold from the fridge

seeds from 4 cardamom pods, crushed
  using a mortar and pestle

1 teaspoon ground cinnamon

2–3 tablespoons confectioners' sugar

1 teaspoon vanilla bean paste

¾ cup smooth blackberry jam

Preheat the oven to 325°F. Grease a 9-inch springform cake pan and line it with parchment paper.

Put the rhubarb slices into a mixing bowl with the 2 tablespoons superfine sugar and 1 teaspoon of the cinnamon and mix well. Set aside.

Put the eggs, remaining superfine sugar, vanilla paste, remaining cinnamon, and ginger into a large mixing bowl and, using a wooden spoon, beat together to mix thoroughly. Add the flour and melted butter and mix well, then mix in the rhubarb pieces, followed by the toasted flaked almonds. Give everything a thoroughly good mix to ensure the ingredients are evenly combined.

Pour the mixture into the prepared cake pan and use a spatula to smooth out the surface. Scatter the raw flaked almonds liberally over the top. Bake until a toothpick inserted into the center comes out clean, about 1 hour. Leave to cool in the pan. Remove the cooled cake from the pan and cut it in half horizontally to make 2 sandwich layers. Use the layer covered in almonds as the top cake layer.

To make the cream filling, put the heavy cream into a mixing bowl with the cardamom, cinnamon, confectioners' sugar, and vanilla paste and beat using an electric mixer until soft peaks form and the cream just holds its shape. If you have time, refrigerate the cream to chill it before using. Spread the cream over the lower half of the cake. Stir the jam to loosen and spoon it over the cream, then sandwich with the top cake layer.

BANANA, COFFEE &
CHOCOLATE CHUNK CAKE

with salted caramel & peanut butter sundae topping

SERVES 10–12

3 large eggs

3 very ripe large bananas, mashed to a fine purée

¾ cup superfine sugar

2 teaspoons vanilla bean paste

1 heaping teaspoon ground cinnamon

2 x 2-tablespoon shots of espresso, cooled

1¾ cups all-purpose flour

1 cup ground almonds

1 teaspoon baking powder

⅞ cup olive oil, plus more for greasing

¼ lb dark chocolate chunks

FOR THE TOPPING

1¼ cup smooth or crunchy peanut butter, at room temperature

1 cup salted caramel spread

¼ lb dark chocolate, shaved or coarsely grated

handful of chopped nuts (optional)

Preheat the oven to 350°F. Select a rectangular cake pan measuring approximately 9 x 13 inches. Grease the pan and line it with parchment paper.

In a large bowl, using an electric mixer, beat the eggs, bananas, and sugar together, then add the vanilla paste, cinnamon, and coffee and blend until the mixture is evenly combined. Add the flour, almonds, baking powder, and olive oil and mix well, then stir in the chocolate chunks. When the mixture is smooth, pour it into the prepared cake pan and bake until the sponge is golden on top and a toothpick inserted into the center of the cake comes out clean, 45–55 minutes. Leave to cool in the pan.

Spread the peanut butter across the surface of the cooled cake. Drizzle over the salted caramel, then cover with the grated chocolate. Refrigerate for 1 hour. Once chilled, sprinkle over the chopped nuts, if using. To serve, remove the cake from the pan and cut into slices. I sometimes like to squirt a dollop of store-bought whipped cream on top, too.

SUMMER
FEASTS

Living in England does mean I spend much of the year longing to feel the warmth of the sun on my face and waiting for the abundance of summer produce to come into play. The joy of sweet-tasting fruits, fresh green vegetables and the sizzling smoke of grilling and barbecuing with friends is the definition of summer in my mind.

We're not so fortunate in England to always have perfect summer weather, but the produce is still plentiful and, overall, we tend to entertain and be entertained more often during the summer months than in any other season. Drinks in hand, we come together to feast on colorful salads, delights from the barbecue both savory and sweet, and plenty of delicious dishes perfect for sharing with a crowd.

I must confess, I don't have a garden, and therefore do not own a barbecue, so I tend to create summer recipes that you can make indoors, rain or shine, which to me evoke the true meaning of summer. You can really play with flavors during the warmer months, because there is an abundance of fresh ingredients to add wonderful little lifts to simple recipes. Everything from herbs, chiles, citrus zests, and even fresh fruits come into their own and deliver the kind of flavor that satisfies everyone.

Summer dishes should be simple and colorful, and they should feed many and satisfy everyone. This chapter reflects what I love to cook and eat most during summertime. (Although to be honest, produce permitting, some of these recipes work beautifully all year-round.) Even if the sun is playing hide and seek with you, you can create dishes that deliver that summer vibe, no matter what the temperature outside may be.

SUMMER FEASTS

MENU

Blackened spatchcock chicken (page 130)

Grilled corn in harissa mayo with feta, mint, cilantro & chile (page 132)

Tamarind & honey pork ribs (page 133)

Vine-baked sea bass with coconut, turmeric, lime, chile & cilantro (page 137)

Orzo & tomato salad with capers & Kalamata olives (page 142)

Accompaniment:
Toasted pita bread or wraps

BUTTERFLIED LEG OF LAMB

with pomegranate salsa

SERVES 4–6

2 lb butterflied leg of lamb

2 tablespoons natural yogurt

2 fat garlic cloves, crushed

2 tablespoons sun-dried tomato paste

1 heaping tablespoon finely chopped thyme

2 tablespoons lightly crushed
coriander seeds

2 tablespoons olive oil, plus more
for cooking

Maldon sea salt flakes and freshly ground
black pepper

FOR THE POMEGRANATE SALSA

1¼ cups pomegranate seeds

½ cucumber, finely diced (to the same size
as the pomegranate seeds)

1 small red onion, very finely diced

1 teaspoon nigella seeds

8 large mint leaves, finely chopped

2 tablespoons pomegranate molasses

1 tablespoon olive oil

Remove the lamb from the refrigerator 20 minutes before you intend to marinate it and ensure it is splayed open and as flat as possible, so that the meat cooks evenly. If there are any sides with much thicker meat, use a small knife to make incisions to open them up and flatten these sides as evenly as possible.

Combine the remaining ingredients in a bowl to make a marinade, seasoning generously with salt and pepper. In a glass or ceramic baking dish large enough to hold the lamb, rub the marinade all over the butterflied lamb leg and really work it in. Cover the dish with plastic wrap and marinate for a minimum of 30 minutes at room temperature, or overnight in the refrigerator, if preferred.

Preheat the oven to 425°F. Line a baking sheet with parchment paper.

Drizzle a little olive oil into a large frying pan set over medium heat. When the oil is hot, place the marinated lamb in the pan with the skin side facing down. Seal the lamb on all sides until nice and brown, without letting it blacken or burn. It should have a nice crust in about 10 minutes. Transfer the lamb to the prepared baking sheet and roast for 15–20 minutes, depending on how you like your meat cooked. I like it very pink and juicy, but if you prefer medium or well done, leave it in for a further 5–10 minutes.

Meanwhile, combine all the ingredients for the salsa in a bowl, stir well, and set aside.

Leave the lamb to rest, covered with aluminum foil, for 10 minutes before carving. Serve with the salsa.

SPICE-MARINATED BEEF KEBABS

2 lb sirloin steak, cut into 1½-inch dice

1 teaspoon sweet smoked paprika

1 teaspoon ground turmeric

2 teaspoons ground cumin

1 teaspoon ground cinnamon

3 garlic cloves, crushed

juice of ½ lemon

Maldon sea salt flakes and freshly ground black pepper

4–5 tablespoons olive oil, plus more as needed

TO SERVE

sliced red onion

natural yogurt

fresh cilantro

pita bread or wraps

Put the beef into a large mixing bowl, add the spices, garlic, lemon juice, a generous amount of salt and pepper and the oil, adding more if necessary to enable the spices to coat the beef pieces. Marinate at room temperature for 1 hour.

I find it easier and less messy to cook the beef pieces in a frying pan and then thread them onto skewers to serve. To cook, heat a large frying pan over high heat. When the pan is hot, place some of the beef pieces in the pan, leaving just a little spacing between them, and cook until a deep brown crust forms, 2–3 minutes on each side. Transfer to a plate, cover with aluminum foil, and leave to rest while you cook subsequent batches. Thread the pieces of beef onto skewers when ready to serve. Serve with onion slivers, yogurt, and herbs in pita breads or wraps.

BLACKENED SPATCHCOCK CHICKEN

SERVES 4

3½ lb chicken (ask your butcher to spatchcock it for you, if preferred)

1 tablespoon cumin seeds

2 teaspoons ground coriander

1 teaspoon ground cumin

seeds from 6 green cardamom pods, finely ground using a mortar and pestle

1 tablespoon pul biber chile flakes

1 tablespoon dried thyme

grated zest of 1 unwaxed lemon

juice of ½ lemon

2 garlic cloves, crushed

1 heaping tablespoon superfine sugar

3–4 tablespoons olive oil

Maldon sea salt flakes and freshly ground black pepper

If you prefer to spatchcock the chicken yourself, place the whole chicken, breast side facing down, on a chopping board and, using a sharp knife, make incisions on either side of the top of the spine. Insert the knife at an incision point, and, carefully using the spine as your guide, pull down the knife to cut away the spine from that side of the chicken. Repeat on the other side to release the spine and discard it (or use it for making stock). Now turn the bird over so that the breast side is facing up and press down firmly on it to flatten the carcass.

Combine the remaining ingredients in a bowl to make a spice paste. In a glass or ceramic baking dish large enough to hold the chicken, rub the paste all over the skin side of the bird. Cover the dish with plastic wrap and leave to marinate for at least 20 minutes or overnight in the refrigerator.

Preheat the oven to 450°F. Line a large baking sheet with parchment paper.

Lay the bird, with the skin side facing up, on the prepared baking sheet. Roast until the chicken is cooked through and the skin is crisp and browned, about 45 minutes. Leave to rest for 10 minutes before serving. (This recipe also works well on a barbecue. Position the chicken over indirect heat and cook for approximately 45 minutes.)

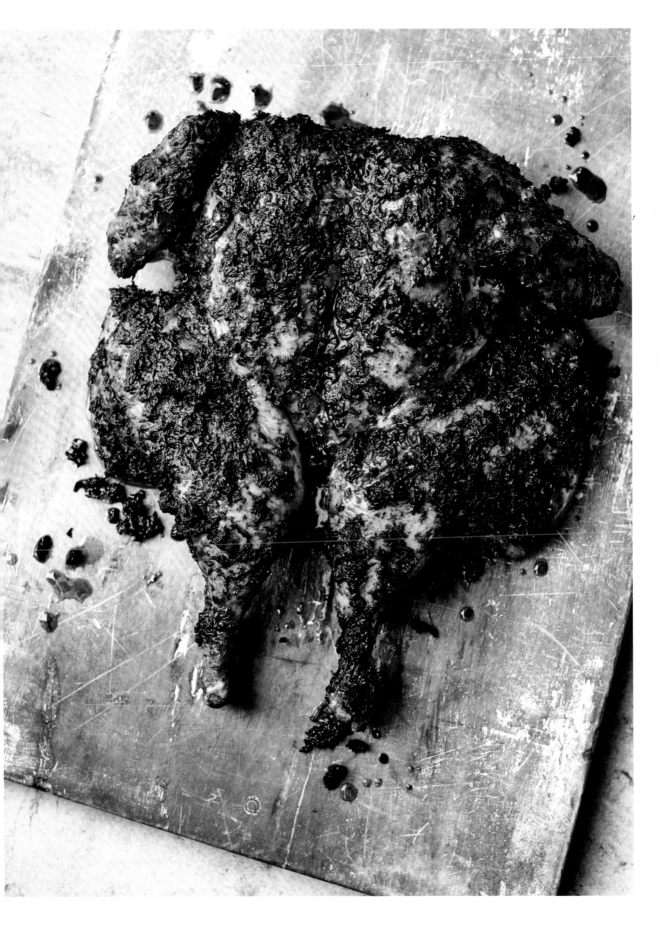

GRILLED CORN IN HARISSA MAYO

with feta, mint, cilantro & chile

MAKES 4

FOR THE HARISSA MAYO
3 tablespoons mayonnaise
1 tablespoon rose harissa
finely grated zest of 1 unwaxed lime
squeeze of lime juice
Maldon sea salt flakes and freshly ground
    black pepper

4 ears corn on the cob
8 oz feta cheese, crumbled into very
    small pieces
1 teaspoon red pepper flakes
handful of finely chopped fresh cilantro
6–8 large mint leaves, roughly chopped

Combine the ingredients for the harissa mayo in a bowl, stir well, and set aside.

Cook the corn in a large pot of boiling water for 10 minutes. Meanwhile, heat a grill pan over medium-high heat. When the cooking time has elapsed, drain the corn, and pat it dry with paper towels.

Place the corn cobs on the hot grill pan and immediately raise the heat to high. Cook, turning occasionally, until char marks appear and the corn is blistering in parts, about 6–8 minutes.

Spread the crumbled feta on a plate. Divide the mayo into 4 portions and spread 1 portion all over each corn cob. Roll the coated cobs in the feta. Sprinkle over the pepper flakes, fresh cilantro, and mint. Serve immediately.

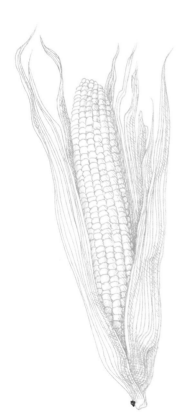

TAMARIND & HONEY PORK RIBS

SERVES 4–6

3½ lb pork ribs

½ cup tamarind paste

5 tablespoons honey

4 tablespoons tomato ketchup

3 fat garlic cloves, crushed

2 tablespoons dark soy sauce

1 tablespoon red pepper flakes

2 teaspoons ground cinnamon

2 teaspoons ground cumin

finely grated zest and juice of 1 unwaxed orange

Maldon sea salt flakes and freshly ground black pepper

Put the pork ribs in a large, deep saucepan and add enough water to generously cover the ribs. Bring the water to a gentle simmer and cook the ribs until tender, about 45 minutes. Drain, then leave to cool completely. Put the cooled ribs into a shallow roasting pan or dish.

Put the remaining ingredients into a bowl, season generously, and stir until to combine well. Pour the marinade over the ribs, ensuring it coats them entirely. You can cook them right away, but it's ideal to marinate them in the fridge for a few hours or overnight to allow the marinade to permeate the meat.

Preheat the oven to 375°F. Line a baking sheet with aluminum foil.

Shake off any excess marinade from the ribs and spread them out on the prepared baking sheet. Roast for 15 minutes, then baste with the marinade and roast for a further 15 minutes. Baste once again, raise the oven temperature to 400°F and cook for a further 10 minutes. Serve immediately.

VINE-BAKED SEA BASS

with coconut, turmeric, lime, chile & cilantro

SERVES 3-6

3 oz fresh coconut, finely grated

finely grated zest of 1 unwaxed lime

1 small bunch (about 1 oz) fresh cilantro, finely chopped

1 long red chile, deseeded and very finely chopped

2 garlic cloves, bashed and crushed

4-inch piece fresh turmeric, finely grated

Maldon sea salt flakes and freshly ground black pepper

olive oil

30–36 vine leaves (allow 5–6 per fillet, depending on size), plus more as required

6 sea bass fillets with skin on (about ¼ lb each)

Preheat the oven to 475°F. Line a baking sheet with parchment paper.

Put the coconut, lime zest, cilantro, chile, garlic, and turmeric in a bowl and season generously with salt and pepper. Add a little drizzle of olive oil and mix well to form a paste.

Using 5–6 barely overlapped vine leaves per fillet, make a sheet of vine leaves on your work surface. Place a sea bass fillet on top with the skin side facing down, as if you were wrapping a present. Divide the topping mixture into 6 portions and spread 1 portion over the flesh of each fillet. Carefully wrap the fillets in their vine leaf sheets, using more leaves as necessary to ensure the fish or topping is sealed well.

Transfer the wrapped fillets to the prepared baking sheet and roast until the fish is cooked through, about 12 minutes. (Test for doneness by unwrapping a fillet; if the flesh is opaque and flakes easily, it's done.) Serve immediately, unwrapping the parcels to serve.

POMEGRANATE, CUCUMBER & PISTACHIO YOGURT

SERVES 6–8

2 cups thick Greek yogurt

1 large banana shallot or 2 small round
    shallots, finely chopped

1 large cucumber, cut into ½-inch dice

1 cup pomegranate seeds, rinsed to remove
    any juice that may color the yogurt

1¼ cups pistachio nuts

1 small bunch (about 1 oz) mint, leaves
    picked and roughly chopped

Maldon sea salt flakes and freshly ground
    black pepper

olive oil

toasted pita bread, to serve

Pour the yogurt into a large bowl and mix in the shallot. Add the cucumber, pomegranate seeds, and pistachios (reserving a little of each for garnish). Add the mint, then fold the everything gently into the yogurt. Season generously with salt and pepper.

To serve, give the mixture a good drizzle of olive oil and scatter over the reserved cucumber, pomegranate seeds, and pistachios. This yogurt is a great dip served with toasted pita bread.

PEACH, FETA & MINT SALAD

with pul biber

SERVES 4–6

4 large peaches, pitted and each cut into
    approximately 10 wedges

1 red onion, thinly sliced into half-moons

extra-virgin olive oil

1 tablespoon pul biber chile flakes

juice of ½ lemon

Maldon sea salt flakes and freshly ground
    black pepper

7 oz feta cheese, crumbled into small pieces

1 small bunch (about 1 oz) mint, leaves
    picked, rolled up tightly, and sliced
    into ribbons

Put the peach slices, onion, a good drizzle of olive oil, pul biber, and lemon juice into a mixing bowl, season generously with salt and pepper and mix well.

Transfer the mixture to a serving dish, then scatter over the feta and mint and serve.

BROWN RICE SALAD

with olives, preserved lemons & apricots

SERVES 6–8

1½ cups whole-grain (brown) basmati rice

1 can (15 oz) lentils

2 cups mixed olives, pitted and halved

1 bunch of spring onions, very thinly sliced
from root to tip

½ lb dried apricots, cut into strips

1 large bunch (about 1¾ oz) fresh cilantro,
roughly chopped

1 large bunch (about 1¾ oz) flat-leaf parsley,
roughly chopped

2 tablespoons ground coriander

8 preserved lemons, deseeded and
finely chopped

1 cup toasted flaked almonds

2 heaping tablespoons sumac

juice of 1 lemon

4 tablespoons honey

good drizzle of olive oil

Maldon sea salt flakes and freshly ground
black pepper

Cook the rice according to the package instructions, then drain and rinse in plenty of cold water to remove all the starch. Drain well in a sieve.

In a large bowl, combine the rice with the remaining ingredients and mix well to serve.

ORZO & TOMATO SALAD

with capers & Kalamata olives

¾ lb orzo pasta

1¼ lb sun-dried tomatoes in oil, drained (oil reserved) and cut into strips

1 lb green beans, trimmed and halved

1½ cups pitted Kalamata olives, roughly halved

1 bunch (about 1¾ oz) flat-leaf parsley, leaves and stems finely chopped

14 oz feta cheese, crumbled into small chunks

¼ lb pine nuts

1½ cups capers in brine, drained

Maldon sea salt flakes and freshly ground black pepper

Cook the pasta according to the package instructions. Rinse thoroughly in cold water and leave to drain for 10 minutes.

Transfer the drained pasta to a large mixing bowl. Add 2 tablespoons of the oil that was drained from the sun-dried tomatoes and mix well to coat the pasta.

Cook the green beans in a large pot of boiling water until al dente, 6–8 minutes, then plunge them into a bowl of cold water to stop the cooking process. Drain well.

Add the cooled, drained green beans to the pasta with the remaining ingredients and mix well. Add a little more of the oil reserved from the sun-dried tomatoes and season very generously with salt and pepper, then mix once more and serve.

BLUEBERRY, LIME &
GINGER CHEESECAKES

MAKES 4

10 ginger cookies, crushed

2 tablespoons unsalted butter, melted

5 oz cream cheese

finely grated zest of 1 unwaxed lime, plus
more to garnish

10 tablespoons heavy cream

8 tablespoons blueberry jam, plus more
to serve (optional)

Put the cookie crumbs in a small bowl and pour over the melted butter. Mix with a fork until the crumbs have absorbed all the butter. Divide the mixture into 4 portions and spoon each portion into a martini glass or tumbler. Pat down gently to compress the crumbs and make a firm base for the cheesecakes. Transfer to the refrigerator.

Put the cream cheese, lime zest, and heavy cream in a large mixing bowl and mix gently until the cream and cream cheese are just combined. Add the blueberry jam and gently stir it through the mixture so it is rippled with swirls of jam but not fully blended.

Remove the glasses from the refrigerator and divide the cheesecake mixture among them. Refrigerate for a minimum of 1 hour, or overnight, before serving. Garnish with lime zest and dollop on a little more jam to serve if desired.

CHARGRILLED PINEAPPLE

with sweet lime & mint yogurt

SERVES 4

1 large pineapple
olive oil
4 tablespoons light brown sugar

FOR THE YOGURT SAUCE
¾ cup Greek-style yogurt
1 small bunch (about ¾ oz) mint, leaves
   picked and finely chopped
finely grated zest of 1 unwaxed lime
good squeeze of lime juice
1 teaspoon confectioners' sugar
1 tablespoon cold water, plus more
   as needed

TO DECORATE
1 long red chile (not a small fiery one),
   deseeded and finely chopped
1 tablespoon light brown sugar (optional)

Heat a grill pan over high heat.

If you prefer, leave the pineapple skin on and simply eat around it when cooked. Otherwise, to remove the skin, first cut off the stem using a large knife, then cut away a circular disk from the base and discard. Now cut away strips of the outer skin from top to bottom until all the skin is removed. Use a small knife to cut away any brown fibrous spots. Cut the pineapple into quarters lengthwise. Cut away the tough core from each quarter.

Brush the cut sides of the pineapple with a little oil to prevent them from sticking. Coat 1 side of each wedge with ½ tablespoon of the brown sugar and place sugar-coated side down on the hot grill pan. Grill, without moving them, until char marks begin to appear, 6–8 minutes. Brush the other sides with oil and coat with sugar, then grill for a further 6–8 minutes, or until equally charred. Transfer the pineapple wedges to serving plates.

Combine the yogurt, mint (reserving a little to decorate), lime zest and juice, and confectioners' sugar in a bowl and mix until smooth. Add the 1 tablespoon cold water to loosen the consistency of the sauce to that of heavy cream, adding more cold water as necessary.

Drizzle the yogurt sauce over the pineapple and scatter over the chopped chiles, brown sugar, if using, and reserved mint and serve.

LIGHTER FEASTS

Every now and then, I overindulge. We all do—it's part of the nature of juggling busy work and home lives. Sometimes when we're feeling down, a little indulgence can cheer us up, and when we're on the go, it can be quick and easy to grab things to eat that aren't terribly nutritious or energy-sustaining.

I'm not much of a diet guru, so don't mistake this chapter for a low-calorie diet section. That's just not my style—I always say I enjoy cake and salad in equal measure. This is simply a collection of recipes that sums up the kind of food I like to eat when I want dishes that are satisfying and a little lighter, and that perhaps don't require much else with them. Some dishes are more virtuous than others; the idea being that they are balanced and delicious, because that is the point really. I dislike the notion that lighter or healthier eating needs to rely on bland, flavor-free, overly simple food, and the misconception that it revolves solely around all that is green or sprouted.

I tend to be a balanced cook, especially when at home. I prefer to cook food with intense flavors, made with simple ingredients boosted with a little spice or citrus and fresh herbs. You'll find in this chapter some of my favorite lighter meals—recipes that are every bit as satisfying as you would expect a good meal to be. We all want dessert, but maybe we don't always want to go the whole hog and indulge in something too exuberant. Simplicity has its beauty, and this chapter, in essence, is more to do with simplicity in content, not necessarily in flavor or process. Fresh flavors, and satisfying and enticing foods, whatever the weather . . . those are the ones we will most likely turn to time and again.

LIGHTER FEASTS

MENU

Yogurt & harissa marinated chicken (page 156)

*Smoked mackerel & quinoa salad with charred asparagus
& cannellini beans (page 159)*

Eggplant rolls with goat cheese, herbs & walnuts (page 162)

Avocado, grapefruit & cashew salad with harissa vinaigrette (page 167)

Pomegranate bulgur wheat salad with sour cherries, almonds & feta (page 168)

Accompaniments:
Crusty bread; tomato salad

CHICKEN & TURMERIC VERMICELLI SOUP

SERVES 4–6

⅓ lb vermicelli rice noodles

3-inch piece fresh ginger, peeled and cut into 3–4 slices

3-inch piece fresh turmeric, halved lengthwise (or 1 teaspoon ground turmeric)

3 garlic cloves, crushed

1 tablespoon red pepper flakes (optional)

2 quarts plus 1 cup cold water (or use fresh vegetable or chicken stock)

Maldon sea salt flakes and freshly ground black pepper

¾ lb shredded cooked chicken (leftovers are ideal)

2 carrots, peeled, halved lengthwise and sliced

3–4 handfuls chopped kale, tough stalks discarded

4 spring onions, thinly sliced from root to tip

1 small bunch (about 1 oz) mint, leaves picked, rolled up tightly and sliced into ribbons

1 small bunch (about 1 oz) fresh cilantro, roughly chopped

Rinse the rice vermicelli under cold running water, then put it in a heatproof bowl and pour over enough boiling water to cover the noodles well. Leave to soak for 10 minutes, then drain the noodles and rinse them under cold running water. Set aside.

Put the ginger, turmeric, garlic, and pepper flakes, if using, in a large, deep saucepan set over medium heat and pour in the water or stock. Season well with salt and pepper and give the mixture a stir, then add the chicken, bring the mixture to a simmer, reduce the heat to low, and simmer gently for 30 minutes. If the soup simmers too aggressively, you may need to add more water and adjust the seasoning.

Remove and discard the fresh turmeric, then add the noodles, carrots, and kale and cook for a further 5 minutes, or until the vegetables are tender. Check and adjust the seasoning as necessary. Remove the pan from the heat, stir in the spring onions, mint, and cilantro. Serve immediately.

YOGURT & HARISSA MARINATED CHICKEN

SERVES 4–6

FOR THE MARINADE

¾ cup thick Greek yogurt

1 small bunch (about 1 oz) fresh cilantro, roughly chopped

2 garlic cloves

2 tablespoons rose harissa

zest of 1 unwaxed lime

juice of ½ lime

1 tablespoon olive oil

Maldon sea salt flakes and freshly ground black pepper

6 large-ish chicken breasts, butterflied

vegetable oil

Put the marinade ingredients in a food processor and season generously with salt and pepper. Blitz the mixture until smooth.

Put the butterflied chicken in a shallow dish. Pour the marinade over the chicken and leave to marinate for a minimum of 30 minutes, or cover the dish with plastic wrap and leave to marinate overnight in the refrigerator. If you have refrigerated the chicken, remove it from the refrigerator 20 minutes before cooking.

Drizzle enough vegetable oil into a large frying pan to just coat the base and set it over medium heat. When the oil is hot, remove the chicken from the marinade, shake off any excess, then add the chicken to the pan. Fry until nicely browned and cooked through, about 8 minutes. Pile the chicken pieces onto a platter and serve hot.

SMOKED MACKEREL & QUINOA SALAD

with charred asparagus & cannellini beans

SERVES 6

12 oz red quinoa

½ lb asparagus tips

olive oil, for brushing

1 lb smoked mackerel fillets (either plain or peppered works well), flaked

1 can (15 oz) cannellini beans, drained

2 tablespoons pul biber chile flakes

½ cup pumpkin seeds

Maldon sea salt flakes and freshly ground black pepper

FOR THE DRESSING

finely grated zest and juice of 1 unwaxed orange

2 tablespoons red or white wine vinegar

1–2 teaspoons Dijon mustard

3–4 tablespoons extra-virgin olive oil

Cook the quinoa according to the package instructions. Rinse thoroughly under cold running water, then leave in a colander to drain.

Put the asparagus tips in a heatproof bowl, pour over enough boiling water to cover them and leave to blanch for 5 minutes. Drain the asparagus, then plunge into a bowl of cold water. Leave to cool in the water, then pat dry with paper towels.

Heat a grill pan over high heat. Brush the cooled asparagus tips with a little olive oil and grill them until char marks appear, about 2 minutes on each side. Cut each asparagus tip into 3 roughly equal pieces and set aside.

Put the quinoa in a large bowl. Add the mackerel, cannellini beans, asparagus, pul biber, and pumpkin seeds and mix well.

Combine the dressing ingredients in a bowl, season with salt and pepper and mix well. Pour the dressing over the salad and toss. Season well with salt and pepper and serve.

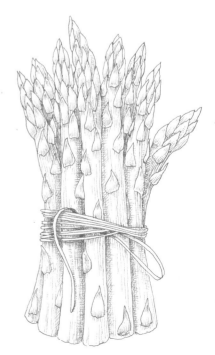

SMOKED SALMON

with capers, olives & preserved lemons

SERVES 4–6

1 lb smoked salmon

1 heaping teaspoon pul biber chile flakes

½ cup nonpareil (tiny) capers

¾ cup pitted mixed olives, sliced crosswise

2 banana shallots, cut into wafer-thin rings

4 preserved lemons, deseeded, 4 roughly chopped and 2 thinly sliced into rounds

3–4 tablespoons extra-virgin olive oil

Maldon sea salt flakes and freshly ground black pepper

Swedish rye crispbreads, to serve

Lay the smoked salmon on a large, flat serving platter. Sprinkle over the pul biber, then scatter over the capers, olives, shallots, and both the chopped and sliced preserved lemons. Drizzle lightly with olive oil and season with salt and pepper. Serve with Swedish rye crispbreads.

EGGPLANT ROLLS

with goat cheese, herbs & walnuts

SERVES 4–6

3 large eggplants, cut lengthwise into
  ¼-inch slices

olive oil, for brushing

10½ oz soft mild goat cheese

1 small bunch (about 1 oz) fresh cilantro,
  finely chopped

1 small bunch (about 1 oz) dill,
  finely chopped

1½ cups walnuts, finely chopped

2 fat garlic cloves, crushed

1 heaping teaspoon ground fenugreek

½ teaspoon cayenne pepper

Maldon sea salt flakes and freshly ground
  black pepper

TO SERVE

½ cup Greek yogurt

6 tablespoons pomegranate molasses

1 cup pomegranate seeds

Heat a grill pan over medium-high heat. Line a plate with
a double layer of paper towels. Brush each slice of eggplant
with olive oil on both sides. When the grill pan is hot, grill the
eggplants until cooked through, about 6 minutes. Transfer to
the paper towel–lined plate to drain excess oil. Leave to cool.

Put the goat cheese in a bowl and add the cilantro and dill
(reserving 1 teaspoon of each chopped herb for garnish). Add
the walnuts, garlic, fenugreek, and cayenne pepper and season
generously with salt and black pepper.

Place 1 tablespoon of the goat cheese mixture on the wider end
of each cooled eggplant slice. If you have filling left over, divide
it among the slices equally. Roll up the eggplant slices around
the filling and place the rolls on a tray or serving plate. At this
point you can refrigerate the rolls so they set and hold their
shapes—remove from the refrigerator 20 minutes before serving.

Put the yogurt in a bowl and stir in just enough water to give
the yogurt the consistency of light cream. Drizzle the yogurt
generously over the rolls, followed by the pomegranate
molasses. Scatter over the pomegranate seeds and reserved
herbs to serve.

SAUTÉED KALE SALAD

with pumpkin seeds, apple, feta & chile sauce

SERVES 6–8

1 lb kale, tough stalks discarded, cut into
    bite-size pieces

olive oil

Maldon sea salt flakes and freshly ground
    black pepper

4 Braeburn apples

juice of ½ lemon

extra-virgin olive oil, for drizzling

1⅓ cups feta cheese, crumbled

Sriracha

⅓ cup pumpkin seeds

Wash the kale, but avoid shaking off all the water from the leaves—the kale will steam in this water later.

Drizzle enough olive oil into a large saucepan to just coat the base and set it over medium–high heat. When the oil is hot, add the kale and season generously with salt and pepper. Stir-fry until just wilted, about 1 minute. Cover the pan with a lid and steam the kale for 2 minutes, shaking the pan (with the lid on) a few times during cooking to keep the kale from sticking to the base of the pan. When the kale is cooked and turns a darker shade of green, transfer it to a bowl and leave to cool for a couple of minutes.

Chop the apple into thin strips. Place the apple strips in a bowl and toss in the lemon juice.

Arrange the kale on a serving platter and drizzle over some extra-virgin olive oil. Scatter the apple and feta over the kale, then drizzle over some Sriracha to taste. Finish with a scattering of pumpkin seeds and serve.

AVOCADO, GRAPEFRUIT & CASHEW SALAD

with harissa vinaigrette

SERVES 4–6

¼ lb arugula

2 large red or pink grapefruit

2 large avocados

¾ cup toasted cashew nuts

Maldon sea salt flakes and freshly ground
    black pepper

½ small bunch (about ⅓ oz) chives, snipped
    into 2-inch lengths

FOR THE HARISSA VINAIGRETTE

2 tablespoons rose harissa

2 tablespoons honey

1 tablespoon red or white wine vinegar

3 tablespoons olive oil

1 teaspoon water

Spread the arugula on a serving platter.

To segment the grapefruit, use a small, sharp knife to cut away the top and bottom of the fruit. Rest the grapefruit on the cut surface, then slice away strips of rind to expose the flesh. When peeled, slice out segments of grapefruit and discard the leftover skin. Repeat with the other grapefruit. If large, slice the segments into half-moon slices.

Halve the avocados, remove the pits, peel away the skin with a knife, then slice each half into strips or chunks. Arrange the avocado and grapefruit over the arugula. Scatter over the cashew nuts and season generously with salt and pepper. Scatter over the chives.

Combine the harissa, honey, vinegar, and oil in a small pitcher, then stir in about 1 teaspoon water to thin out the dressing a little. Season with salt and pepper. Drizzle the dressing over the salad and serve immediately.

POMEGRANATE BULGUR WHEAT SALAD

with sour cherries, almonds & feta

SERVES 6–8

3½ cups pomegranate juice
(100 percent pomegranate; I use Pom)

8 oz bulgur wheat

1 tablespoon honey (optional)

olive oil

Maldon sea salt flakes and freshly ground
black pepper

1 small bunch (about 1 oz) dill, finely
chopped

1 small bunch (about 1 oz) flat-leaf parsley,
finely chopped

2 long red chiles, deseeded and very
finely chopped

1 cup sliced almonds

1 cup dried sour cherries (sweetened)

8 oz feta cheese, finely crumbled

Put the pomegranate juice in a saucepan and bring to a boil over medium heat. Add the bulgur wheat and simmer until the juice is mostly absorbed by the grains, 20–25 minutes. If you wish to offset the sharp flavor, add the honey while the bulgur wheat is cooking. Leave to cool.

Fluff the cooled bulgur grains with a fork. Drizzle over a little olive oil and season well with salt and pepper. Stir well, then add the chopped dill and parsley, chiles, sliced almonds, and sour cherries, mixing them in with a fork to prevent them from sticking together. Last, add the feta and fork it through, then serve.

TIP

Don't be put off by the color of the bulgur wheat—different brands of pomegranate juice will have different strengths of color—go by the flavor of the overall dish.

WATERMELON, RADISH & WATERCRESS SALAD

with pickled cucumber

SERVES 6–8

FOR THE PICKLED CUCUMBER
1 cucumber
Maldon sea salt flakes
1 teaspoon superfine sugar
3 tablespoons rice wine vinegar

FOR THE DRESSING
1½ tablespoons honey
½ teaspoon cayenne pepper
½ teaspoon ground cinnamon
olive oil
reserved cucumber pickling liquid
   (see method)
Maldon sea salt flakes and freshly ground
   black pepper

½ watermelon, balled using a melon baller
½ lb radishes, quartered or
   roughly chopped
¼ lb watercress
nigella seeds, to garnish

Halve the cucumber lengthwise, then scoop out and discard the seeds. Cut the cucumber halves into thin slices. Put them in a large mixing bowl and season generously with salt. Add the sugar and rice wine vinegar. Using your hands, mix everything together, ensuring the cucumber slices are well coated in the mixture. Leave to stand for 15–20 minutes. Toss the cucumbers once again in the juice that has formed in the bowl, then drain the cucumbers, reserving 2 tablespoons of the liquid in a separate bowl. Set both aside.

To make the dressing, add the honey, cayenne pepper, cinnamon, a good drizzle of oil, and some salt and black pepper to the 2 tablespoons reserved cucumber pickling liquid and mix well.

Arrange the watermelon, radishes, watercress, and pickled cucumber slices on a serving platter. Scatter over some nigella seeds, and serve with the dressing.

POMEGRANATE &
ROSEWATER JELLY CUPS

MAKES 4

4 sheets of gelatin

1¾ cups pomegranate juice
    (100 percent pomegranate; I use Pom)

2 tablespoons alcohol-free rosewater

⅓ cup superfine sugar

⅔ cup pomegranate seeds

In a small bowl, soak the gelatin sheets in cold water until soft, about 5 minutes.

Meanwhile, set a small saucepan over low heat and pour in the pomegranate juice and rosewater. Stir in the sugar. Heat the mixture gently, just until the sugar dissolves, then immediately remove the pan from the heat.

Add the soaked gelatin sheets, 1 at a time, to the pomegranate juice mixture and stir until each leaf is dissolved before adding the next. Leave the mixture to cool until lukewarm, about 20 minutes.

Pour the liquid into 4 glasses or cups. Sprinkle the pomegranate seeds over each cup. Leave to cool completely, then refrigerate the jelly cups overnight or for a minimum of 4 hours before serving.

RASPBERRY & PISTACHIO
FROZEN YOGURT POTS

MAKES 6

⅓ lb fresh raspberries

1 teaspoon vanilla bean paste

1¼ cups Greek yogurt

¾ cup pistachio nut slivers or chopped
    pistachio nuts

2 tablespoons honey

TO DECORATE

6 frozen raspberries

¼ cup pistachio nut slivers

Using a blender, purée the raspberries, vanilla paste, yogurt, pistachios, and honey together until smooth. Divide the mixture into 6 dessert cups or small bowls, then freeze overnight.

Remove the pots from the freezer 10 minutes before you want to serve them. Crumble over a frozen raspberry on top of each pot, then sprinkle over a few pistachio slivers just before serving.

SPECIAL OCCASIONS

In selecting a collection of recipes for all-important occasions, I wanted to place the emphasis on special-feeling dishes—recipes for times when you want to impress people or treat friends and loved ones to food with a little more thought and depth given to it than usual. These types of recipes usually signify that more effort than usual has gone into making them.

The following recipes are dishes that will make a menu feel celebratory. While there are a few dishes in this chapter that—although they may not be terribly complicated— may take some time to cook or prepare, there are also simpler dishes to help create perfect balance, not only in terms of menu creation but also in terms of time spent in the kitchen. I am particularly proud of the showstopping Fig & Rose Millefeuille (page 203), because it looks as though you've slaved away for hours, but it couldn't be simpler to prepare. The very last thing I want to do when I am cooking a special meal is to spend the entire time in the kitchen, missing out on the fun—the whole point of entertaining is to be with your loved ones.

Personally, I feel the most special occasions include convivial, simple, and abundant food on the table, surrounded by the kind of people I can genuinely feel at ease with, even if they've all showed up dressed glamorously for the party while I only manage to make it to the table in a onesie, smelling of roasted meats and fried things . . . those are the best kind! With a little thought and some easy prep you can achieve so much, and I hope this chapter inspires you to host your own special occasions more often.

SPECIAL OCCASIONS

MENU

Griddled lobster tails with barberry, garlic, lime & chile butter (page 187)

Jumbo shrimp with tomato, dill & fenugreek (page 188)

Beer-roasted pork shoulder with plum sauce (page 182)

Saffron roast potatoes (page 190)

---

*"Confetti" rice with zucchini, eggplant, peppers,
pine nuts, golden raisins & herbs (page 197)*

Accompaniment:
Wilted chard or greens

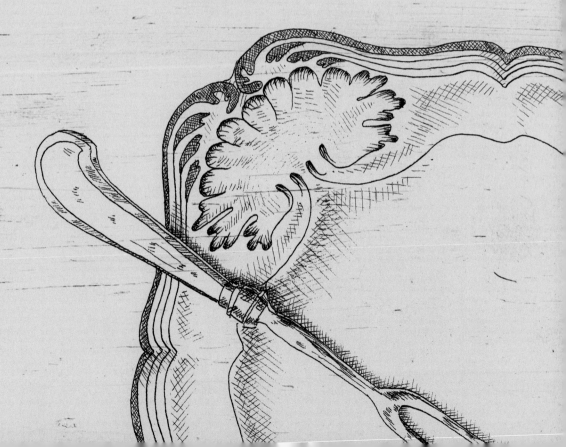

SPICED LAMB HOT POT

SERVES 4–6

1 tablespoon cumin seeds

6 cardamom pods, lightly cracked

vegetable oil

2 large onions, thinly sliced into half-moons

2 lb diced leg of lamb

1 large garlic bulb, cloves peeled and left whole

8 shallots, peeled and left whole

2 large carrots, peeled and cut into ½-inch dice

1 teaspoon ground cumin

1 teaspoon ground ginger

1 teaspoon ground cinnamon

½ teaspoon cayenne pepper

1 teaspoon English mustard powder

2 tablespoons all-purpose flour

Maldon sea salt flakes and freshly ground black pepper

2¼ cups chicken, lamb or vegetable stock

1½–1¾ lb red potatoes, unpeeled, thinly sliced

4 tablespoons unsalted butter, melted

sprinkling of thyme leaves

Preheat the oven to 325°F.

Heat a large dutch oven or other large flameproof pot over medium heat. When the pot is hot, add the cumin seeds and cardamom pods and toast until the spices release their aroma, about 2 minutes, stirring occasionally to prevent burning.

Pour enough oil into the pot to coat the base. When the oil is hot, add the onions and fry until translucent and the edges start to brown, 6–8 minutes. Add the meat and cook for a few minutes, stirring to coat in the oil and cumin seeds. Add the garlic cloves, shallots, and carrots and stir for a couple of minutes, then add the ground cumin, ginger, cinnamon, cayenne pepper, mustard powder, and flour and a generous seasoning of salt and black pepper. Mix well, then stir in the stock.

Arrange the potato slices on top of the meat, slightly overlapping them. Brush with the melted butter, sprinkle with thyme leaves, and season again with salt and pepper, then cover the pot with a lid and transfer to the oven to cook for 1½ hours.

Take the hot pot out of the oven and remove the lid. Raise the oven temperature to 425°F. Return the pot to the oven, uncovered, and cook until the potatoes are golden brown, about 30–40 minutes. Serve immediately.

BEER-ROASTED PORK SHOULDER

with plum sauce

SERVES 4–6

3½–4½ lb shoulder of pork

olive oil

4 teaspoons dried wild oregano
 (or regular oregano)

3 teaspoons celery salt

3 teaspoons English mustard powder

3 teaspoons coarse black pepper

3 teaspoons ground coriander

2¾ cups pale ale or lager

FOR THE PLUM SAUCE

1¼ lb plums, pitted and roughly chopped

3 teaspoons ground coriander

1 teaspoon cayenne pepper

Maldon sea salt flakes and freshly ground
 black pepper

½ small bunch (about ½ oz) tarragon,
 leaves finely chopped

1 cup water, plus more as needed

Preheat the oven to 325°F. Line a large roasting pan with parchment paper.

Place the pork shoulder in the prepared pan and, if any string has been used to tie it together, remove it. Score the skin, then drizzle over some olive oil and rub it into the meat.

Mix the oregano, celery salt, mustard powder, black pepper, and coriander together in a small bowl. Scatter the mixture all over the pork and use your hands to rub it in, especially on the underside and deep into the skin on top. Pour the beer around the pork and add a little splash on top, ensuring you don't rinse off the spice mixture. Roast until cooked through, about 4 hours. Check the pork after 3 hours and, if it is browning excessively, cover it with a double layer of aluminum foil for the remaining cooking time.

If the skin has not crisped up when the cooking time has elapsed, remove the pork from the oven and raise the oven temperature to 425°F. Using tongs, carefully peel the skin off the meat and lay it flat on a rack set over a baking sheet. Roast the skin until crispy, 10–15 minutes. Meanwhile, cover the pork loosely with foil and leave to rest for about 30 minutes.

To make the sauce, put the plums, ground coriander, and cayenne pepper in a saucepan set over medium-low heat and season with salt and black pepper. Sweat the plums for about 15 minutes, mashing them until they soften and are cooked. Stir in the chopped tarragon and add the water, raise the heat to medium and cook gently until the sauce has reduced to a gravy-like consistency, about 10 minutes. Add more water if necessary to reach your preferred sauce consistency.

Carve or shred the pork and serve with the crackling and plum sauce.

SPICE-ROASTED QUAIL

with sour cherry sauce

½ teaspoon coarse black pepper

1 teaspoon ground cumin

½ teaspoon ground turmeric

pinch of ground cloves

olive oil

4 quails (about ⅓ lb each), giblets removed

FOR THE SOUR CHERRY SAUCE

¼ lb dried sour cherries (sweetened),
  very finely chopped

½ teaspoon ground cinnamon

Maldon sea salt flakes and freshly ground
  black pepper

honey

2 tablespoons salted butter, softened

Preheat the oven to 425°F. Line a baking sheet with parchment paper.

Mix the dry spices together in a small bowl. Drizzle a little olive oil over each quail, then divide the dry spice mix among the quails, sprinkling it over. Use your hands to rub the spices into the oil and coat the birds all over, then place them on the prepared baking sheet. Season generously with salt, then roast for 30–35 minutes.

Meanwhile make the sauce. Put the sour cherries in a small saucepan set over medium-low heat, pour in just enough boiling water to cover them and bring to a gentle simmer. Add the cinnamon and cook until the mixture has a sauce-like consistency, 6–8 minutes, adding a little more water if needed. Season well with salt and pepper, and add a little honey to sweeten the sauce to your taste, then add the butter and stir until melted. When you're happy with the flavor, stir well and leave to simmer until the quails are cooked.

Remove the quails from the oven, cover loosely with aluminum foil and leave to rest for 6–8 minutes. Serve the quails whole or halved, with the sauce.

GRIDDLED LOBSTER TAILS

with barberry, garlic, lime & chile butter

SERVES 4–8

5 tablespoons salted butter, softened

finely grated zest of 1 unwaxed lime

2 tablespoons barberries, very finely
chopped or blitzed in a food processor

2 garlic cloves, crushed

2 tablespoons finely chopped fresh cilantro

1 heaping teaspoon red pepper flakes

Maldon sea salt flakes and freshly ground
black pepper

4 lobster tails (about ¼ lb each), fresh or
frozen (thawed if frozen)

Combine the butter with the lime zest, barberries, garlic, cilantro, pepper flakes, and a generous amount of salt and pepper until evenly blended. Refrigerate until needed.

Heat a grill pan over high heat.

Using a large, sharp knife, split each of the lobster tails in half lengthwise. Place the split tails, with their shells facing down, on the hot grill pan—the shells will heat up and cook the lobster meat inside. Remove the flavored butter from the refrigerator and dot two-thirds of it across the exposed lobster flesh. When the butter begins to melt, use a pastry brush to baste the lobster meat with it. Leave to cook for 2 minutes, then turn the lobster tails so that the flesh sides are facing down and cook for 45 seconds. Flip them over to check if the meat is opaque and cooked through. Dot the meat with the remaining butter and, when it begins to melt, transfer to a serving platter and serve immediately.

JUMBO SHRIMP

with tomato, dill & fenugreek

SERVES 4

olive oil

1 large onion, halved and thinly sliced into half-moons

3 fat garlic cloves, crushed

1 teaspoon ground turmeric

1 can (14½ oz) chopped tomatoes

4 large tomatoes, each cut into 8 pieces

1 heaping tablespoon tomato paste

3 tablespoons (or 5 if frozen) dried fenugreek leaves

1 tablespoon fenugreek seeds, toasted and ground to a powder using a mortar and pestle

1 teaspoon ground cinnamon

1 heaping teaspoon red pepper flakes

1 teaspoon superfine sugar

Maldon sea salt flakes and freshly ground black pepper

1¾ lb large raw shrimp, or raw peeled shrimp

2 tablespoons salted butter

½ small bunch (about ½ oz) dill, roughly chopped

toasted bread or rice, to serve

Drizzle enough oil into a large frying pan to just cover the base and set it over medium heat. When the oil is hot, add the onion and fry until translucent and the edges start to brown, 6–8 minutes.

Add the garlic to the pan and cook for 30 seconds, then add the turmeric and cook for a further minute. Next add the canned and fresh tomatoes, tomato paste, fenugreek leaves, ground fenugreek seeds, cinnamon, pepper flakes, and sugar and stir well to blend the spices into the sauce. Reduce the heat to low, season with salt and pepper, cover partially with a lid and simmer gently for about 30 minutes. Stir occasionally to prevent it from burning.

Heat a separate frying pan over high heat. When the pan is hot, add the shrimp and fry for 30–40 seconds on each side, to seal. Remove the shrimp from the frying pan and stir them into the sauce to finish cooking. Add the butter and stir until incorporated, then remove the pan from the heat, stir in the dill (leaving some for garnish), scatter more dill on top and serve with bread or rice.

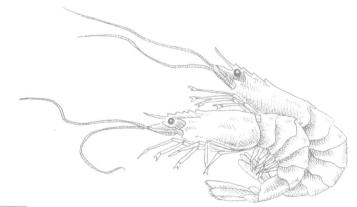

SAFFRON ROAST POTATOES

SERVES 4–6

1 pinch Iranian saffron

2 generous pinches of Maldon sea salt flakes, plus more to season

2–3 tablespoons boiling water

3 lb roasting potatoes

2 tablespoons table salt

6 tablespoons vegetable oil or light olive oil

Preheat the oven to 375°F. Line a baking sheet with parchment paper. Line a plate with a double layer of paper towels.

Using a mortar and pestle, grind the saffron with the sea salt flakes to a fine powder. Add the boiling water and set aside to infuse.

Peel the potatoes, then trim any larger potatoes to ensure all the potatoes are roughly the same size. Put them in a pan of cold water to rinse off the excess starch, then drain. Bring a large pot of water to a boil, add the table salt, and parboil the potatoes for 8–10 minutes.

Drain the parboiled potatoes in a colander and leave to stand for 5 minutes to allow the excess moisture to evaporate. Shake the colander to help fluff up the potatoes and rough up the edges. Transfer the potatoes to the prepared baking sheet.

Combine the saffron solution with the oil, mix well, and pour the mixture over the potatoes. Season generously with sea salt flakes. Using a large metal spoon, turn the potatoes in the saffron oil to coat them. Season again, then roast for 30 minutes. Remove the baking sheet from the oven, give it a good shake, then bake for a further 45 minutes, or until crispy. Transfer to the paper towel–lined plate to drain excess oil. Serve immediately.

CHARRED CAULIFLOWER STEAKS

with tahini, harissa honey sauce & preserved lemons

SERVES 6

2 large cauliflowers

3 tablespoons rose harissa

4 tablespoons honey

1 tablespoon olive oil, plus more for frying

1 teaspoon ground cinnamon

Maldon sea salt flakes and freshly ground
   black pepper

4 tablespoons tahini

6 tablespoons Greek yogurt

good squeeze fresh lemon juice

TO SERVE

6 preserved lemons, deseeded and thinly
   sliced into rounds

generous handful toasted flaked almonds

½ small bunch (about ½ oz) flat-leaf
   parsley, roughly chopped

Cut away any outer leaves from the cauliflower, then cut each cauliflower into 4 slices of equal thickness. On each slice, cut from the outer edges of the cauliflowers, trim and shave away enough of the curves to create flat surfaces, so that the slices cook evenly.

Combine the harissa, honey, olive oil, and cinnamon in a small bowl, season with salt and pepper, and mix well. Brush or rub the mixture over the cauliflower slices.

Drizzle a little oil into a large frying pan set over medium heat. When the oil is hot, fry the cauliflower slices until they are cooked through and charred nicely on both sides, 6–8 minutes on each side. Blackening will occur as the spice paste is not only dark but also contains sugar (in the honey), which will burn naturally. This is part of the flavor of the dish and nothing to be worried about. (Alternatively, roast the cauliflower slices in a preheated oven, at 425°F, for 20–25 minutes.)

Meanwhile, mix the tahini with the yogurt and lemon juice in a bowl, season generously with salt, then stir in a little lukewarm water, 1 tablespoon at a time, until the mixture has a sauce-like consistency.

Transfer the cauliflower steaks to serving plates. Drizzle over the yogurt sauce and any remaining marinade, then scatter over the preserved lemon slices, toasted almonds, and parsley to serve.

TIP

To make this a vegan recipe, substitute coconut or soy yogurt for the Greek yogurt.

PAN-ROASTED PEPPERS

with a sweet harissa glaze

SERVES 6

1 tablespoon cumin seeds

olive oil

6 large peppers (I like to use a mix of red, yellow, and orange), cut vertically into ¼–⅓-inch-thick strips

1 teaspoon ground cinnamon

2 tablespoons rose harissa

3–4 tablespoons honey

Maldon sea salt flakes and freshly ground black pepper

1 tablespoon red wine vinegar

½ small bunch (about ½ oz) flat-leaf parsley, roughly chopped, plus more to garnish

Heat a large frying pan over medium-high heat, add the cumin seeds and toast until they release their aroma and begin to brown a little, about 1 minute, shaking the pan and taking care not to let them burn. Drizzle in enough oil to coat the base of the pan and raise the heat. Add the peppers and cook, stirring occasionally, until they begin to soften and brown around the edges, 8–10 minutes.

Add the cinnamon, harissa, and honey to the pan and season generously with salt and pepper. Last, add the vinegar and stir to coat the peppers in the sauce. Cook for 2 minutes, then remove the pan from the heat, stir in the parsley, and adjust the seasoning if desired. Scatter with chopped parsley and serve as a topping for bruschetta or as a condiment for cheese. They are also great alongside chorizo sausages.

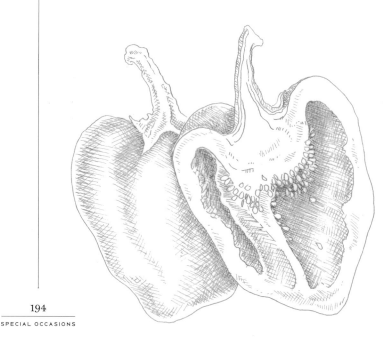

"CONFETTI" RICE

with zucchini, eggplant, peppers, pine nuts,
golden raisins & herbs

SERVES 4–6

olive oil

1 large onion, very finely chopped

1 large eggplant, very finely diced

1 red pepper, very finely diced

1 green pepper, very finely diced

2 zucchini, very finely diced

¼ lb golden raisins

¼ lb pine nuts

Maldon sea salt flakes and freshly ground
black pepper

1 small bunch (about 1 oz) dill,
finely chopped

1 small bunch (about 1 oz) flat-leaf parsley,
finely chopped

2¼ cups basmati rice

3 tablespoons salted butter, cut into
small pieces

Drizzle a generous amount of olive oil into a large frying pan set over medium-high heat. When the oil is hot, add the onion and fry until translucent and the edges start to brown, 6–8 minutes. Add the eggplant and fry until it starts to turn golden, then add the peppers and zucchini and continue to fry for a further 1 minute. Remove the pan from the heat. Stir in the raisins and pine nuts and season generously with salt and pepper. Stir in the dill and parsley and set aside.

Cook the rice according to the package instructions. Fluff the grains with a fork, then tip the rice into a large mixing bowl.

Stir the butter into the vegetable mixture. Pour the mixture over the rice. Using a large spoon, fold the vegetable "confetti" through the rice without mashing or crushing the rice. Adjust the seasoning if needed and serve immediately.

TIP

When preparing the vegetables it is important to chop them all into very small dice and all the same size. This attention to detail will ensure the finished dish looks more refined.

BLACKBERRY & APPLE
MUFFIN SANDWICHES

with rosemary & orange cream

MAKES 12

3 large eggs

1⅛ cup superfine sugar

1 tablespoon vanilla bean paste

2 teaspoons ground cinnamon

1¾ cups all-purpose flour

2 teaspoons baking powder

1 cup salted butter, melted

1 large Braeburn apple, cut into ½-inch dice

¼ lb blackberries, halved

**FOR THE ROSEMARY
& ORANGE CREAM**

1 heaping teaspoon rosemary leaves

3 tablespoons superfine sugar

1¼ cups heavy cream

finely grated zest of 1 unwaxed orange

Preheat the oven to 350°F. Line a 12-cup muffin pan with paper liners.

Put the eggs, sugar, vanilla paste, and cinnamon into a large mixing bowl and beat together. Stir in the flour and baking powder, then add the melted butter and mix until smooth. Fold in the apple and blackberries—don't worry if you mash them slightly.

Divide the mixture among the lined muffin cups and bake until the muffins are deep golden brown and a toothpick inserted into the centers of the cakes comes out clean, about 40 minutes. When cooked, remove them from the pan and leave to cool.

To make the cream, blitz the rosemary leaves with the sugar in a spice grinder until the mixture turns into a fine dust. Transfer the mixture to a large bowl and add the cream and orange zest. Using an electric mixer, beat until soft peaks form and it just holds its shape.

When the muffins are cool, remove them from the paper cases and slice them in half horizontally. Spread the cream over the lower half of each cake, then sandwich together with the top halves and serve.

CHERRY, DARK CHOCOLATE & MINT PARFAIT

SERVES 6

2 large eggs, separated

⅓ cup superfine sugar

1 teaspoon vanilla bean paste

1¼ cups heavy cream

½ small bunch (about ½ oz) mint, leaves picked, rolled up tightly and roughly chopped

6 oz frozen pitted cherries, thawed and roughly chopped (reserve any excess juices)

¼ cup dark chocolate chunks

Line a 9 x 5 x 3–inch loaf pan with a double layer of plastic wrap, leaving plenty of plastic wrap overhanging the pan.

Put the egg yolks, sugar, and vanilla paste in a large mixing bowl. Using an electric mixer, beat the mixture until pale, thick, and creamy.

In a separate bowl, whip the cream until soft peaks form, then gently whisk the cream into the egg mixture.

Wash the mixer beaters, then beat the egg whites in another bowl until stiff peaks form. Using a wooden spoon or a spatula, gently fold the beaten egg whites through the egg mixture until evenly combined.

Add the mint, cherries (and any juice), and dark chocolate chunks to the bowl and carefully fold them into the mixture.

Transfer the mixture to the prepared loaf pan. Cover the parfait with the overhanging plastic wrap and freeze for at least 6 hours, or overnight.

To serve, remove the parfait from the freezer and leave to soften for a few minutes. Unfold the plastic wrap on top and use the edges to lift the parfait out of the pan. Flip it onto a serving tray or chopping board, discard the plastic wrap, and use a flat-bladed knife to smooth the surface, dipping the knife into hot water occasionally to clean it and achieve a smooth finish. Leave to soften slightly for 10–15 minutes, then slice and serve immediately. This is great served with wafers, nuts, and dark chocolate sauce, or sandwiched in brioche buns.

TIP

You can use fresh cherries for this dish instead of frozen. Use roughly the same quantity of pitted cherries and soften them briefly in a pan with 1 heaping tablespoon superfine sugar, then leave to cool.

FIG & ROSE MILLEFEUILLE

with pistachios & a passion fruit & honey cream

SERVES 6

1 sheet of frozen all-butter puff
  pastry, thawed

2 tablespoons superfine sugar

2½ cups heavy cream

2–3 tablespoons honey,
  plus more to serve

pulp and seeds from 3 large or 4 small
  passion fruits

½ small bunch (about ½ oz) mint, leaves
  picked, rolled up tightly and sliced
  into ribbons

4–5 fat black figs, thinly sliced into about
  5 slices

½ cup pistachio nut slivers or roughly
  chopped pistachio nuts

3 tablespoons dried edible rose petals,
  lightly ground using a mortar and pestle

Preheat the oven to 400°F. Line a baking sheet with parchment paper.

Gently prick each side of the pastry about 20 times, working evenly and neatly across the sheet. Cut the pastry sheet into 3 equal-size rectangles, then lay them on the prepared baking sheet. You need to prevent them from rising more than ½ inch, so place an inverted baking sheet over them. Bake for 20 minutes, then remove the most attractive-looking rectangle (to use as the top layer) and set it aside to cool. Return the remaining pastry rectangles, covered with the inverted baking sheet, to the oven and bake until deep golden brown and crisp, about 7 minutes longer. Remove from the oven and leave to cool.

When the first rectangle removed from the oven is cool, brush the top with lukewarm water, then scatter over the sugar. Return to the oven and bake until crisp and golden brown, and the top is nicely glazed, about 7 minutes. Leave to cool.

Whip the cream with the honey until nice and thick, then drizzle in the passion fruit pulp and seeds and stir gently to marble it through the cream, ensuring you don't fold it through completely.

To assemble, place a cooked pastry rectangle on a serving platter to serve as the base. Spread one-quarter of the cream on top. Scatter over one-third of the mint and arrange half of the fig slices on top of the mint and cream. Scatter over one-third of the pistachios. Spread another quarter of the cream on top of the pistachios, then sprinkle over one-third of the rose petal powder. Now place the second pastry rectangle on top and repeat the layering process. Place the sugar-crusted pastry rectangle on top, then scatter over the remaining mint, pistachios, and rose petals. Give the millefeuille a final drizzle of honey and serve.

COMFORT
FOOD

Comfort food is often defined as warming, cheese-laden pasta-, potato-, rice- or bread-based dishes, or pies, casseroles, and other hearty fare. I guess this entirely depends on the comforting moment you associate with that dish—the significant person who once made it for you, or maybe a warm holiday memory. However, comfort food can mean one thing to one person and something entirely different to another. Although I absolutely love cheesy, creamy, carb-heavy warming winter dishes, for me comfort food is usually anything that I can eat that makes me smile and allows me to be utterly comfortable while eating it!

I have a terrible habit of eating in bed. Not eating at bedtime, but the physical act of eating in my bed. Since I started writing books, I spend an inordinate amount of time testing in my kitchen late into the night, so as a treat I really enjoy the luxury of reclining in bed, perhaps like a much less glamorous version of a Roman empress, holding a bowl or plate of food and enjoying it in the sanctuary of my own bed—that, to me, is the ultimate comfort.

Comfort aside, the food itself has to be pretty spectacular. A salad of just leaves never really provides me with much comfort, it must be said, but add some shredded meat, feta, chiles, a little spice, and some croutons and suddenly we are out of Saladville and into Comfort Town territory. Mostly, comfort food is bold in flavor, whether simple or complex, and requires no formality to enjoy. These are recipes that you can happily indulge in—or overindulge in—and you won't be sorry later, as they satisfy and give you a little of what you fancy. Because, as we all know, a little of what you fancy does you good.

COMFORT FOOD

MENU

Lamb kofta roll (page 215)

Lamb, plum & preserved lemon stew (page 219)

Spicy beef noodles with green beans (page 220)

Cardamom & coconut dhal with turmeric & nigella seeds (page 223)

Freekeh, tomato & chickpea pilaf (page 227)

Accompaniments:
*Cooked basmati rice; natural yogurt with fresh mint;
radish & celery salad*

CAULIFLOWER, ANARI, BLACK PEPPER & THYME QUICHES

MAKES 12

1 cauliflower
olive oil
2 teaspoons freshly ground black pepper,
   plus more to taste
handful of thyme leaves, finely chopped
1 ⅔ cups heavy cream
2 ½ oz dry Anari cheese, finely grated
Maldon sea salt flakes
3 sheets of filo pastry
3 large eggs

Chop the cauliflower (florets and stem) into ½-inch cubes and put them in a large frying pan set over medium heat. Fry for a couple of minutes to extract any excess moisture, stirring frequently. Drizzle in a little olive oil, continuously moving the cauliflower around the pan to avoid it browning. Add the pepper, chopped thyme, and heavy cream and stir well. Just as the cream begins to bubble, remove the pan from the heat and stir in the grated cheese. Season the mixture with salt and pepper and leave to cool completely.

Preheat the oven to 400°F. Brush the cups of a 12-cup muffin pan generously with olive oil.

Cut each filo pastry sheet into 8 squares, roughly about 4 ½ inches square. Overlap 1 pastry square with another to make an 8-pointed star. Push the stars into the cups of the muffin pan.

When the cauliflower mixture has cooled, mix in the eggs thoroughly. Distribute the mixture equally among the 12 pastry cases, then bake until the tops are nicely golden and a toothpick inserted into the center of the quiches comes out clean, 30 minutes. Serve warm.

TIP

If you can't find Anari cheese, substitute feta or goat cheese instead.

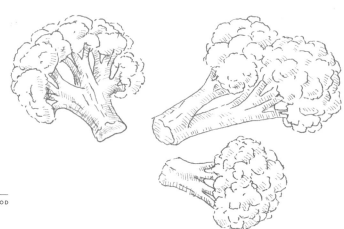

BLACK GARLIC, TAPENADE, & FETA ROLLS

MAKES 10–12

3¾ cups white bread flour, plus more for dusting

¼ oz package of instant yeast

1 teaspoon superfine sugar

Maldon sea salt flakes and freshly ground black pepper

1¼ cups warm water

2 tablespoons olive oil, plus more for drizzling

1–1¼ cups black olive tapenade

2 heads of black garlic, cloves thinly sliced

2–3 tablespoons dried wild thyme

8 oz feta cheese, crumbled

Combine the flour, yeast, and sugar in a large mixing bowl and crumble in 2–3 good pinches of sea salt flakes and a grinding of pepper. Pour 1 cup plus 2 tablespoons of the water into the flour mixture, along with the olive oil, then bring the dough together first using a fork, then with your hands. If it feels dry, mix in just enough of the remaining water to just dampen it; otherwise, drizzle over a little olive oil to keep it moist.

Knead the dough for a couple of minutes, then leave to stand for 10 minutes. Knead it again for 1 minute. Repeat this process once more: knead the dough for 2 minutes, leave to stand for 10 minutes, then knead again for 1 minute. Put the dough in a clean bowl, cover the bowl with a clean kitchen towel and leave it somewhere warm to rise until it has almost doubled in size, about 1½ hours.

Line a baking sheet with parchment paper. Dust your work surface with flour.

Punch down the dough in the bowl, punching it a couple of times with your fist. Transfer the dough to a floured work surface and, using a rolling pin, roll it out into a rectangle measuring about 12 x 16 inches. Spread the tapenade across the surface of the dough, then place the black garlic slices evenly across the tapenade. Scatter over the wild thyme and crumbled feta. Roll up the dough to make a long 16-inch roll. Using a sharp knife, cut the roll into 10–12 slices.

Lay the slices on the prepared baking sheet, ensuring there is 1¼ inches between each slice to allow them to expand while cooking. Cover the baking sheet loosely with plastic wrap and leave to proof until the slices have almost doubled in size, about 30 minutes.

Meanwhile, preheat the oven to 400°F. When the rolls are ready, bake until golden brown, 35–40 minutes. Transfer to a wire rack and leave to cool before serving.

LAMB KOFTA ROLL

SERVES 4–6

1 lb minced lamb

3 eggs

1 small bunch (about 1 oz) flat-leaf parsley, finely chopped

2 tablespoons pul biber chile flakes

4 fat garlic cloves, crushed

3 tablespoons tomato paste

1 onion, very finely chopped

Maldon sea salt flakes and freshly ground black pepper

1 sheet of frozen all-butter puff pastry, thawed

1 tablespoon nigella seeds

TO SERVE

¾ cup Greek yogurt

Sriracha

Preheat the oven to 400°F. Line a baking sheet with parchment paper.

Combine the meat with 2 of the eggs, the parsley, pul biber, garlic, tomato paste, and onion in a large bowl. Season generously with salt and pepper. Mix the ingredients with your hands until the mixture becomes a smooth, evenly mixed paste.

Unroll the pastry. Lay the meat in a long sausage shape across the center of the pastry. Fold the pastry over the sausage and pinch the pastry around the meat to seal it. Transfer to the prepared baking sheet.

Beat the remaining egg and use it to brush the pastry all over. Sprinkle over the nigella seeds. Bake until the pastry is deeply golden brown and crispy, about 25 minutes.

Transfer the roll to a serving platter and slice to serve. Serve hot with yogurt and Sriracha (or other chile sauce) on the side.

PARSNIP & APPLE SOUP

SERVES 6–8

vegetable oil

2 onions, chopped

4-inch piece fresh ginger, finely grated

3 teaspoons fennel seeds, toasted and finely ground using a mortar and pestle

seeds from 6 green cardamom pods, finely ground using a mortar and pestle

2 lb parsnips, peeled and cut into chunks

6 apples, peeled, cored, and cut into chunks

2 qt vegetable stock

Maldon sea salt flakes and freshly ground black pepper

6 tablespoons cream-style horseradish

pumpkin seed oil, to garnish (optional)

Pour enough vegetable oil into a large saucepan to cover the base, add the onions and fry over medium heat until softened, 6–8 minutes. Add the ginger, ground fennel, and cardamom seeds and mix well, then stir in the parsnips and apples. Sweat for a few minutes without browning until the parsnips have softened.

Pour in the stock, then season with salt and pepper. Simmer until the parsnips can be easily mashed, about 45 minutes. Stir in the cream-style horseradish, then remove the pan from the heat and leave to cool until just warm. When cooled, use an immersion blender to purée the soup to your preferred consistency.

Drizzle over a little pumpkin seed oil if desired, season with pepper, and serve.

HARISSA-INFUSED
LEG OF LAMB

with fenugreek & lime

SERVES 4–6

FOR THE MARINADE

¾ cup Greek yogurt

4 teaspoons fenugreek seeds, toasted and crushed using a mortar and pestle

3 tablespoons rose harissa

3 kaffir lime leaves

2 teaspoons turmeric

4 large garlic cloves, crushed

finely grated zest of 1 unwaxed lime

juice of ½ lime

2 tablespoons ghee or vegetable oil

Maldon sea salt flakes and freshly ground black pepper

4½ lb leg of lamb

Line a baking sheet with parchment paper.

Combine the marinade ingredients in a bowl, season generously with salt and pepper, then stir together to form a smooth paste.

Cut 3 slashes on the top of the lamb leg and a couple more on the underside of the leg. Place the meat on the prepared baking sheet, then massage the paste into the meat, especially in the slashes and bone areas. Leave the meat to marinate in the refrigerator overnight or, if you are pushed for time, for a minimum of 1 hour.

Preheat the oven to 425°F. Put the lamb in the oven and immediately reduce the temperature to 375°F. Roast until the flesh takes on a nice pink color, about 1 hour. If you prefer your lamb slightly more cooked, increase the cooking time by 20 minutes. You can also slow-cook the lamb at 350°F, for 4 hours—check after 3 hours and, if necessary, cover the meat with aluminum foil to prevent burning, for a tender, fully cooked result.

Cover the leg of lamb loosely with aluminum foil and leave to rest for 10 minutes before serving.

LAMB, PLUM & PRESERVED LEMON STEW

SERVES 6-8

vegetable oil

2 large onions, roughly chopped

1¾ lb lamb neck, cut into chunks

Maldon sea salt flakes and freshly ground black pepper

2 handfuls dried fenugreek leaves

¼ lb fresh cilantro, finely chopped

¼ lb flat-leaf parsley, finely chopped

6 plums, halved and pitted

8 preserved lemons, halved and deseeded

Set a large saucepan or dutch oven over medium heat and drizzle in a generous amount of oil. When the oil is hot, add the onion and fry until translucent and the edges start to brown, 6–8 minutes. Add the diced lamb and cook, stirring frequently, for a few minutes to seal it without browning, then season well with salt and pepper. Stir in the dried fenugreek leaves, ensuring the lamb is well coated in them (add more oil if you need it), then add the cilantro and parsley and stir-fry until the herbs have completely wilted, reduced in volume, and lost their bright green color, 12–15 minutes.

Pour in enough boiling water to just cover all the ingredients, then reduce the heat to low. Cook for 2 hours, stirring occasionally. Add the plum halves and cook for a further 45 minutes.

Stir in the preserved lemon halves and season to taste. Cook for a further 5 minutes to heat through. If not serving straight away, leave the stew to cool completely, then refrigerate (see tip). Gently reheat the stew and serve alongside plain basmati rice.

TIP

This stew is at its best and even more delicious when made the day before you serve it. You can also substitute pork neck for the lamb.

SPICY BEEF NOODLES

with green beans

SERVES 6–8

1 lb minced beef (15 percent fat)

8 oz salted peanuts

1 lb flat rice noodles (about ½-inch wide)

vegetable oil

1 large head of garlic, cloves bashed and thinly sliced

2 teaspoons ground cumin

1 teaspoon ground cinnamon

1 lb trimmed green beans, cut into 1-inch pieces

4 tablespoons light tahini

2–3 tablespoons rose harissa

Maldon sea salt flakes and freshly ground black pepper

1 bunch of spring onions, thinly sliced from root to tip

1 small bunch (about 1 oz) fresh cilantro, finely chopped

Remove the minced beef from the refrigerator and let it come to room temperature.

Heat a large frying pan over medium-high heat. When hot, add the peanuts and toast until they start to blacken in parts but not all over, 5–6 minutes. Transfer to a bowl and set aside. Reserve the frying pan (without washing it).

Rinse the noodles under cold running water—I find this prevents them from sticking together during cooking. Drain in a colander.

Put the noodles in a large saucepan set over high heat and add enough boiling water to generously cover the noodles. Cook according to the package instructions or to your preference. Reserve 2 large cupfuls of the cooking liquid for making the sauce, then rinse the noodles under cold running water. Drain, then return the noodles to the pan and set aside.

Meanwhile, pour just enough oil into the frying pan you used to toast the peanuts to coat the base of the pan. Heat the oil over medium heat, then add the minced beef and break it down with a wooden spoon as quickly as possible to avoid clumping. Add the garlic, cumin, and cinnamon and stir-fry until the beef turns brown and is starting to crisp on the edges. Stir in the green beans and fry for a further 5 minutes. Last, add the tahini and rose harissa, season with a generous amount of salt and pepper and stir in a little cold water to thin out and loosen the mixture, if needed, to prevent the tahini from thickening.

Pour the beef mixture into the pan containing the noodles. Add a cup of the reserved noodle-cooking liquid and mix well until incorporated. If, like me, you like a brothy dish you can add the second cup of cooking water. Check the seasoning. Mix in the spring onions and cilantro and serve, garnished with the charred peanuts.

CARDAMOM & COCONUT DHAL

with turmeric & nigella seeds

2 teaspoons cumin seeds

2 teaspoons coriander seeds

2 black cardamom pods

seeds from 7 green cardamom pods

2 teaspoons fennel seeds

2 tablespoons ghee or vegetable oil, plus more as needed

2 onions, finely chopped

5 fat garlic cloves, crushed

3–4-inch piece fresh turmeric, finely grated or 1 heaping teaspoon ground turmeric powder

1 lb red lentils

1¾ oz desiccated coconut

13½ fl oz–can coconut milk

Maldon sea salt flakes and freshly ground black pepper

4 tablespoons salted butter

TO GARNISH

2 tomatoes, diced

1 red onion, finely chopped

½ small bunch (about ½ oz) fresh cilantro, chopped

2 teaspoons nigella seeds

Heat a large frying pan over medium-high heat, add the cumin seeds, coriander seeds, black cardamom pods, green cardamom seeds, and fennel seeds and toast, shaking the pan until they release their aroma and begin to brown a little, about 2 minutes, taking care not to let them burn. Set aside the black cardamom pods, then crush the remaining toasted spices using a mortar and pestle.

Return the crushed spices to the pan. Raise the heat to medium-high. Add the ghee or oil to the spices, then add the onions and fry for about 6 minutes, then add the garlic and fry for 1 minute, stirring to ensure it does not burn. Add the grated turmeric (or ground turmeric powder) and fry until the onions are soft, 1–2 minutes.

Add the lentils and desiccated coconut to the saucepan (and a little more ghee or oil, if the pan looks dry). Stir well, ensuring they are coated in the onion, spice, and ghee mixture. Cook, stirring, for 1–2 minutes, then pour in the coconut milk and add the toasted black cardamom pods. Top up with enough water to completely cover the contents of the pan. Season well with salt and pepper.

Bring to a boil, then cover the pan with a lid, reduce the heat to low and simmer for about 45 minutes, stirring occasionally to prevent sticking. Check the liquid level from time to time—if the liquid is being absorbed too quickly, add a little more water. If the liquid level seems too high, raise the heat level and remove the pan lid to reduce the liquid volume in the pan.

Just before serving, discard the black cardamom pods, then stir in the butter. Serve garnished with the tomatoes, red onion, fresh cilantro, and a sprinkling of nigella seeds.

SPICED POTATOES

with garlic chips & turmeric yogurt

SERVES 4–8 AS A SIDE

1½ lb waxy potatoes, such as fingerling, Anya or Charlotte, halved lengthwise

extra-virgin olive oil

finely grated zest of 1 unwaxed lemon

2 teaspoons cumin seeds

1–1½ teaspoons red pepper flakes

1 tablespoon coarse black pepper

ghee or vegetable oil

Maldon sea salt flakes and freshly ground black pepper

FOR THE TURMERIC YOGURT

¾ cup Greek yogurt

extra-virgin olive oil

3-inch piece fresh turmeric, finely grated

1 small bunch (about 1 oz) mint, leaves picked, rolled up tightly and thinly sliced into ribbons

6 fat garlic cloves, bashed, thinly sliced, and fried into garlic chips

Bring a large saucepan of water to a boil. Add the potatoes and parboil them until the potatoes are almost cooked but still firm in the centers (use a toothpick or knife to check this), about 10 minutes. Drain and rinse the potatoes, then pat them dry, put them in a bowl, and leave to dry. When dry, drizzle a little extra-virgin olive oil into the bowl and add the lemon zest, cumin seeds, pepper flakes, and pepper. Toss to coat the potato halves well.

Pour enough ghee or vegetable oil into a large frying pan to generously coat the base and set it over medium heat. When the oil is hot, add the potatoes with their cut sides facing downward. Fry them slowly until the potatoes have a deep golden crust on them, 8–10 minutes on each side. (Alternatively, roast them at 425°F, for 35–40 minutes if you prefer.) Transfer the potatoes to a serving platter and season well with salt.

Meanwhile, season the yogurt with salt and pepper and stir in a little olive oil. Mix the grated turmeric loosely into the yogurt, swirling it to give a marbled effect.

Scatter the mint and crispy garlic chips over the fried potatoes, and serve with the turmeric yogurt.

FREEKEH, TOMATO & CHICKPEA PILAF

SERVES 6

2 tablespoons cumin seeds

olive oil

4 large onions, 1 diced and 3 halved and
  very thinly sliced into half-moons

2 tablespoons tomato paste

2¼ cups freekeh

4 tablespoons unsalted butter

1 can (14½ oz) chopped tomatoes

1 can (15 oz) chickpeas, drained

1⅔ cups chicken or vegetable stock

1 cup water

Maldon sea salt flakes and freshly ground
  black pepper

vegetable oil

TO GARNISH

¾ cup Greek yogurt

handful of chopped cilantro or parsley

TIP

**To make this a vegan recipe, omit the
butter, and substitute coconut or soy
yogurt for the Greek yogurt.**

Heat a large frying pan over medium-high heat, add the cumin seeds and toast, shaking the pan until they release their aroma and begin to brown a little, about 2 minutes, taking care not to let them burn.

Add a drizzle of olive oil to the pan, add the diced onion, and fry until softened, 6–8 minutes. Add the tomato paste and dissolve it into the onion mixture, adding a little more oil if needed, then add the freekeh and butter and stir well until the freekeh is evenly coated in the onion mixture and the butter has melted. Stir-fry for 1 minute, then add the canned tomatoes and chickpeas and mix well.

Pour in the stock and the water and season with a generous amount of salt and pepper. Cover the saucepan with a lid, reduce the heat to low, and cook for 20–25 minutes without disturbing the pan. Remove the pan from the heat and set aside, leaving the lid on.

Meanwhile, make the fried onions for a garnish. Line a plate with a double layer of paper towels. Pour enough vegetable oil into a saucepan to fill it to a depth of ½ inch and heat over high heat. Add the sliced onion and fry until golden brown and crispy, 8–10 minutes (avoid stirring or they will start to caramelize). Remove the fried onions with a metal slotted spoon and transfer to the paper towel–lined plate to drain.

Add half the fried onions to the freekeh and, using a fork, gently comb through the freekeh to stir in the onions and fluff up the grains and chickpeas. Arrange the freekeh mixture on a wide, flat platter. Dot with the yogurt and scatter the remaining fried onions and cilantro or parsley on top. This is also good drizzled with your favorite hot sauce.

WHITE CHOCOLATE, CARDAMOM & MACADAMIA SQUARES

MAKES 9

2 large eggs

⅔ cup unsalted butter, melted (or ⅔ cup oil, if you prefer), plus more for greasing

¼ cup light muscovado sugar

¾ cup superfine sugar

seeds from 6 cardamom pods, finely ground using a mortar and pestle

2 teaspoons ground ginger

finely grated zest of 1 unwaxed orange

1¾ cups all-purpose flour

7 oz white chocolate, melted

2¾ oz macadamia nuts, halved

light cream, to serve

Preheat the oven to 400°F. Grease an 8-inch square brownie or cake pan and line it with parchment paper.

Using a wooden spoon or an electric mixer, beat the eggs, melted butter, and sugars together in a large mixing bowl until the mixture is smooth. Add the ground cardamom seeds, ground ginger, and orange zest and mix well. Blend in the flour until the mixture is smooth. Mix in the white chocolate and blend again until smooth, then fold in the macadamia nuts.

Pour the mixture into the prepared pan. Bake for 25–30 minutes, or until set on top—they should still be a bit gooey inside. During the last few minutes of the cooking time, prepare a shallow pan with iced or cold water to extend halfway up the sides of your cake pan. When the cake is baked, plunge the pan into the water, making sure no water enters the pan—this will stop the cooking process and leave you with a nice fudgy center. Leave the pan to sit in the cold water until the cake is completely cool. Cut into 9 squares and serve with light cream.

TIP

If making this treat the night before serving, keep refrigerated until ready to serve.

DOUGHNUT FRITTERS

with cinnamon-orange sugar

MAKES 20-24

FOR THE SPICED SUGAR
1 cup superfine sugar
finely grated zest of 2 unwaxed oranges
2 teaspoons ground cinnamon

FOR THE DOUGHNUT FRITTERS
2 cups all-purpose flour
1 teaspoon baking powder
pinch of Maldon sea salt flakes
1½ cups boiling water
4 tablespoons unsalted butter, melted
vegetable oil

First, prepare the spiced sugar. Mix the sugar, orange zest, and cinnamon in a shallow bowl. Cover with plastic wrap and set aside.

To make the fritters, sift the flour, baking powder, and a good pinch of salt into a mixing bowl and make a well in the center. Pour the boiling water into a measuring cup with a spout and stir in the melted butter. Pour the mixture into the flour and combine quickly to make a sticky dough. Leave to rest for 10 minutes.

Pour enough oil into a large, deep saucepan to fill to a depth of about 2 inches. Bring the oil to a frying temperature (to test, drop a pinch of dough into the oil: if it immediately bubbles gently, the oil is at the right temperature). Meanwhile, line a baking sheet with paper towels.

Using a metal teaspoon, scoop up a spoonful of dough. Push it off the spoon and carefully into the hot oil. Repeat until the pot is almost full, ensuring there are not too many in the pot to avoid them sticking together. Fry until deep golden brown, 3-4 minutes on each side. (If the fritters brown too quickly, the oil may be too hot—reduce the heat slightly if this happens.) When cooked, use a slotted spoon to transfer the fritters to the paper towel–lined baking sheet to drain any excess oil, then roll each fritter in the spiced sugar to coat. Repeat with the remaining dough, then serve immediately.

TIP

To make this a vegan recipe, substitute light olive oil for the butter.

ADDITIONAL MENU IDEAS

VEGAN FEAST

Pomegranate & eggplant salad
(page 52)

Charred cauliflower steaks
(page 193)

Cardamom & coconut dhal
with turmeric & nigella seeds
(page 223)

Freekeh, tomato & chickpea pilaf
(page 227)

Doughnut fritters with
cinnamon-orange sugar
(page 230)

PERFECT PICNICS

Pea pastizzi (page 26)

Tomato & olive salad with
za'atar & buttermilk dressing
(page 57)

Orzo & tomato salad
(page 142)

Eggplant rolls with goat cheese,
herbs & walnuts (page 162)

Blackberry & apple sandwiches
(page 198)

Cauliflower, anari, black pepper &
thyme quiches (page 210)

CASUAL FOOD WITH FRIENDS

Goat cheese & filo pies with orange, pistachio & oregano (page 17)

Ultimate chicken shawarmas (page 73)

Harissa skirt steak sandwiches (page 75)

Grilled corn in harissa mayo with feta, mint, cilantro & chile (page 132)

Lamb kofta roll (page 215)

Blueberry, lime & ginger cheesecakes (page 145)

HEARTY FAMILY FOOD

Chicken, pistachio & black pepper curry (page 42)

Spiced green bean & tomato stew (page 113)

Garlic, fenugreek & cumin flatbreads (page 115)

Spiced lamb hot pot (page 181)

Banana, coffee & chocolate chunk cake with salted caramel & peanut butter sundae topping (page 119)

INDEX